People of Promise
How to Be an Authentic Believer

J. Daniel Lupton

D0089661

MAINSTAY CHURCH RESOURCES
WHEATON, ILLINOIS

CONTENTS

Introduction

ACKNOWLEDGMENTS

Every successful venture is a team effort. Writing and publishing a book is a relay race filled with the invaluable contributions of many significant players. My deepest appreciation to these who took the baton and passed it on:

• My wife, Nancy, who has endured both my solitary hours at the keyboard and my frequent interruptions with: "Let me read you something I've just written." How much does Nancy love me? She loves me enough to smile through a first draft.

• Randall Mains, CEO of Mainstay Church Resources, for entrusting me with writing the guidebook for the 50-Day Spiritual Adventure "Promises Worth Keeping." He could have chosen a more famous author—his confidence in me is humbling.

• Promise Keepers for permission to adapt their well-known seven promises for a wider audience, or in this case, readership. They've demonstrated the grace to see the promises as belonging to Christ and his wider kingship.

• David Mains, Director of The Chapel of the Air Ministries and author of more than twenty books, for reviewing and advising on each chapter. His affirmation, even pleasure, with the book's development spurred me on from introduction to final page.

• Marian Oliver, Mainstay Church Resources Director of Product Development, for all legal arrangements, liaison efforts, and general goodwill.

• Janet Burroughs Woodward for permission to use her poem and Rudy Gehr for consent to use his story. For my wife, children, granddaughter, sister, cousins, nieces, nephews, assorted relatives, and many friends from church and life whose names and stories appear without permission. I'll ask forgiveness later.

• Kerry Tanke, friend and daily coworker, for expert editing of every paragraph, sentence, and word. She's rescued many a dangling participle and my honor in the process.

• Laurie Mains, Mainstay Church Resources editor, for taking my disks and printouts, performing the final fine-tune editing, and handing me back a book. How this happens is still one of the mysteries of life.

And you—the baton is now in your hand. When invited to speak at a convention or church, I often assure the contact person that I'll "exalt Jesus Christ, honor God's Word, and do your people some good and no harm." That's my warrant to you with *People of Promise*. If some impulse drives you to contact me, I can be reached by e-mail at LupConsult@aol.com.

"Gold! Gold Rush gold—the gold that opened California to a flood of settlers—was discovered near here! Let's take the afternoon and scout this region." Larry Clouse had invited my wife, Nancy, and me to a mountain tour with his wife, Elizabeth. We had chosen a week in late June for our first Sacramento visit. The daily afternoon temperature was in the triple digits Fahrenheit; any excuse for an escape from valley heat to mountain relief would have been a quick sell at 107 degrees. I wondered how hot it was in the desert when Jesus was tempted by Satan. His courage was growing more impressive to me all the time.

After a stop at the Placerville tourist entrapment site, Larry suggested we go higher to a mountaintop logging camp restaurant where "steaks come on turkey platters, and pancakes are piled so high they sometimes topple over." Pavement changed to dirt, hold-your-breath-and-pray switchbacks. During those occasional moments when my eyes weren't closed with fear, the view was spectacular.

"I don't know where we are, but I think I know where we're going," Larry offered. That sounded like my life journey, and a sudden, heavenly arrival seemed imminent.

The mountain terrain leveled out at the top. Piles of logs stretched on for a mile or more on each side of the road until it ended at the crude shack Larry had referred to as a restaurant. I ruled out linen table-cloths from my expectations. The diner was filled with loggers, any eleven of whom could have whipped the Chicago Bears. Paul Bunyan's genes lived on in these men. We ate logger meals, which we justified by saying we'd take a mountain hike afterwards. Can you walk off 5,000 calories in 20 minutes?

Our hike followed a logger trail, then a deer trail, until we came to a mountain stream, which mean-dered in little pools storing energy for its coming down-ward rush. We paused, gazing into crystal-clear water. Larry grabbed my arm, pointing into the water. "Dan, do you see them?"

> *Larry stood on the bank watching the spectacle of Dan Lupton making a fool of himself over gold.*

"See what?" I asked, straining to find something of interest.

"Those shiny specks, flakes—gold! *Gold!*" Larry's voice was so excited it was hushed. "Dan, you've got to get a jar or envelope. You can have the gold. Get in there."

Jumping into the water, I fervently tried to make those gold specks stick to my fingertips. Larry stood on the bank watching the spectacle of Dan Lupton making a fool of himself over gold.

Then he began to laugh. From the moment we left Placerville, Larry had been setting up this practical joke. It wasn't by chance that we left the logging trail to follow the deer path. "Dan, that's not gold.

That's just fool's gold. The real gold was panned out of here more than 100 years ago." This was followed by more peals of hysteria: "I wish I had a movie camera of you going after the gold!" followed by more laughter, which was starting to have an irritating rasp in my ears.

That was twenty years ago. To this day, when life gets a little dreary for Larry, he retells this moment. His grandchildren are frightened as he doubles over in mirth. "Papa, are you okay?"

"Yes," he gasps for air, "but you should have seen Dan going for the gold!"

The link between gold and iron pyrite (fool's gold) is interesting. There is no relationship except casual appearance. Gold is valued for its authentic purity, beauty, and rarity. Fool's gold is scoffed at, ridiculed as an imposter. Which is more plentiful, real gold or fool's gold? Fool's gold, of course. The abundance of fool's gold, however, fails to diminish the value of genuine gold, and in some measure may enhance it.

Nancy and I had fun that day with Larry and Elizabeth. But putting your faith in an imposter is no joy at all. Not when the issues of life are at stake. Not when "the fake" is an employer, elder, president, or spouse. Marriages, investments, careers, and eternal destinies are gained or lost through whom we trust. We require transparent integrity and authenticity in relationships, religious beliefs, and promises.

Jesus was authentic. Crowds came to see him because of his miracles, but those who chose to follow him did so because they believed in his authenticity. Jesus was himself, no matter who he was with or where he was. Shakespeare wrote, "All the world's a stage, and every man an actor." That doesn't apply to Jesus. He didn't act a part—not in public or private, not at the temple or in a home. "Anyone who has seen me," he said, "has seen the Father" (John 14:9). He was not covering up hidden thoughts or agendas. He was so transparently authentic that you could see God through him. Jesus is the real thing. He is the eternal "I am," not the "I am pretending to be."

> Jesus is the real thing. He is the eternal "I am," not the "I am pretending to be."

Jesus wanted his followers to be authentic, too. At the last sacred meal Jesus shared with his disciples, inauthenticity was on his mind. One person in the room was an imposter. "One of you shall betray me," he said (Matthew 26:21, KJV). This declaration broke his companions' hearts. "They were exceedingly sorrowful," and they began to ask one after another, "Lord, is it I?" (verse 22).

Each of the Twelve (except Judas, and possibly even he) detested hypocrisy. Yet each knew the weakness of his own heart. There, in the presence of Jesus, each disciple inspected his own life: "Lord, is it I? Could I be the fool's gold Christian among us?"

This book is based on a universal application of the well-known promises of the Promise Keepers movement. While Promise Keepers maintains its unique calling and focus—ministry to men—the organization has granted me permission to present these seven promises to anyone who longs for authenticity in life. These seven promises are great guidelines for us to be all we can be, all God wants us to be. They are for women, teens, and children, as well as for men. They are for singles, couples, and families. They are for you, if you want to live life to the fullest and not just pass into the next day. Instead of a person of compromise, you can be a person of promise.

People of promise are those who live up to their potential, daily finding fresh grace to fulfill God's purposes. People of promise sift life's pursuits until they determine those of the highest value, and they pledge to make these excellencies the priorities of life.

As we explore the seven promises, we'll have some fun together. We'll make promises together. We'll find God's help and patience. And from time to time, we'll ask ourselves, "Lord, is it I? How am I doing in this area? Am I real or fake, fool's gold or 24-karat?" Let's go for the pure gold.

An adaptation of the seven promises reads:

With God's help, I promise to . . .

1) Nurture a growing intimacy with the Lord Jesus Christ.
2) Cultivate vital friendships that encourage me to keep my promises.
3) Practice purity in thought and action.
4) Make family relationships a priority.
5) Support the ministry of my church and pastor.
6) Identify and address the hidden prejudices of my heart.
7) Influence my world with the love of Christ.

There, that didn't sound so masculine, did it? But in God's timing and grace, he chose to address these principles to men first.

At Beaver Creek, Colorado, I stood at the bottom of the ski slope welcoming the victors in an all-star race that kicked off the state's winter season. This was good-natured competition filled with joking and laughter. Everyone was a winner, especially the television network sponsor! Our best Olympic skiers competed in this charity event against the best of yesteryear. Nineteen-year-old champions raced for the gold side-by-side against forty-nine-year-old champions from an earlier era. The old-timers (most wouldn't be pleased with that term) were each given a handicap of a one- to three-second head start on the younger and faster competitors. They needed to be out of the gates early so they wouldn't be overly embarrassed at the finish line.

Most men will admit they needed a headstart on the Promise Keeper themes. But this race for authenticity. integrity, and holistic holiness is for women and children as well as for men. Whether panning or racing, we are all going for the gold of an authentic life pleasing to God as well as to us. That's why we're people of promise.

CHAPTER 1

The Ultimate Knowledge

*With God's help, I promise to nurture
a growing intimacy with the Lord Jesus Christ.*

I thought I was lost, but Santaquin was too tiny a town in which to be lost. At the end of a lane in front of an irrigation ditch at the back side of the property, I found her small house trailer. A cottonwood tree was shedding in the breeze, the air was seasonally warm, and the door was open behind the screen. Within sat a beautiful elderly lady with her Bible open on the kitchenette table. Mabel Kearns's cheerful words and beaming smile welcomed me, a stranger, into her quarters. "Please come in. You've caught me in the middle of my morning quiet time. Every day I spend two hours with Jesus. How can I help you?"

My business was no longer as interesting as meeting a retired woman who spent two hours a day with Jesus. Her face glowed with the radiance Christ brings to life. I wondered if this was how Moses looked after he sampled the glory of God. Mabel was dressed as though she had an important appointment. But this appointment was with Jesus. White, sunlit hair framed her countenance, enhancing all Jesus was doing with her by his presence.

Two weeks earlier, my wife and I had packed our

1

belongings into a U-haul truck that was as large as Mabel's trailer. We had driven from Michigan to Utah, where we believed God was calling us to plant a church. Nancy and I had studied maps and demographics and had made inquiries. There were reports of a Christian family or two and a widow in Payson, twenty miles south of Provo, who might be interested in starting a church. In 1970, Payson was a town of five thousand citizens. Mabel lived in Santaquin, an even smaller village of about one thousand, five minutes south of Payson along the Wasatch mountain front.

> *I felt like a bit player in a program being directed by Jesus and his friend Mabel. It was a most wonderful moment of being humbled.*

When I shared my story, she listened and gave Jesus the glory. "Every morning I read the Bible, Old and New Testaments. Then I sit here and worship him with thanksgiving and hymns like I would sing if we had a church. Next I go through my prayer list." This was a three-ring notebook filled with well-worn pages. I wanted to be on that prayer list. "One of my daily requests has been for God to send someone to start a church. You are God's answer to these prayers." Nancy and I had been on her list for a couple of years. Only our names were lacking.

Correcting my initial impression of her simple life, I realized this was a woman of means after all. The old axiom proved true: "It isn't what you know, but who you know." Mabel knew Jesus well enough to transplant the Luptons from Michigan to a town they hadn't heard of a few weeks before. We were playing a small part in Jesus' and Mabel Kearns's scheme. A few minutes earlier, I had thought I was the significant one: "I'm here to start the church you need." Now I felt like a bit player in a program being directed by Jesus and his friend Mabel. It was a most wonderful moment of being humbled.

I had come to offer something and had found a woman who had everything. She possessed that which people long for and some seek desperately. Mabel had a faith that was at once both relevant and transcendent. Her God met her inner spiritual and emotional needs while visiting with her daily.

Why was I surprised that Jesus made a temple out of a trailer? I don't mean any indignity with the term *trailer*. Her home was more than a travel camper but less than what you picture as a mobile home. Mabel had fewer of this world's goods than most of us expect, and more of what we desire than anyone I had ever met. She had contentment, peace, joy, love, security, hope, and a smile, all gained through an intimacy with the Lord Jesus Christ. Besides, Mabel's quarters were luxurious compared with Jesus' first night in an innkeeper's stable. Jesus has always been comfortable in the homes of the poor.

Authenticity Through Godliness
Like Abraham, Mabel Kearns found a way to be happy in the Lord and built an altar wherever she landed. Dr. Warren Wiersbe taught that Abraham lived both in a tent and at an altar: a tent to show he was a pilgrim passing through this world and an altar for worship and communion with God. Mabel's trailer was her tent, and her kitchen table was her altar.

Wherever you are, you can build an altar and know the Lord Jesus Christ. *"We have an altar* from which the priests in the Temple on earth have no right to eat" (Hebrews 13:10, italics added). Jesus now invites us back to a spiritual altar, the place where we meet him, receive his strength, give him our prayers, and praise him. This altar can be anywhere as long as you see Christ as crucified, buried, risen, and interceding for you in heaven.

Mabel wasn't pretentious; her altar was not for show. She was simply an authentic Christian. Ten years ago I heard a message on authenticity. The fact that I remember it makes it noteworthy. I've preached some messages I've forgotten, some others have forgotten, and some I wish I *could* forget. Once in a while we are blessed with a sermon experience that we remember forever.

"God made man and woman in his image and likeness," the preacher said. "Therefore, the more godly the man or woman, the more real the person is. An ungodly man is scarcely a man at all. An ungodly woman is scarcely a woman." That message on authenticity will never leave me. Here is another way to say it: A boat is most boatlike in the water. A boat that never leaves the garage is scarcely a boat at all. It may look like a boat, but it doesn't function as a boat.

> God made man and woman in his image and likeness. Therefore, the more godly the man or woman, the more real the person is.

"God created people in his own image; God patterned them after himself; male and female he created them" (Genesis 1:27). The more godly we are, the more human we are becoming, the more we are functioning as our Lord intended when he designed us. Don't settle for less; don't compromise your privilege as a human being.

God sees himself in you. That may be a hint as to

why he can't stop loving you. God poured himself into each of us. You who have borne and raised children have poured your own nature, temperament, and inclinations into your sons and daughters. That happened at conception. In the years that followed, you continued to pour your love, wisdom, and energy into your children.

There is more than a bit of a mom and dad in each boy or girl. Whether young children live by parental instruction or their own rebellion, they will never shake the fact that they bear a remarkable likeness to their parents. When I look in the mirror, I see my father. Nancy knew my dad when we first dated, so she was forewarned how I would look at this stage of my life. I also think like my parents and have moods like them. I don't like lima beans any more than they did. Dad and Mom live on in me.

God looks at you and sees a bit of himself. More than a bit: He sees a great deal of himself in you because he made you in his image. Those who believe in Jesus and respect his commandments and Word grow in godliness and become more like him. Those who have an altar of worship and a relationship with Jesus are becoming godly in the fullest sense and, with that, becoming fully human.

God believes in you more than you believe in yourself. He sees your value and your potential. You can become a godly person of promise. Will you resolve now: *I promise, with God's help, to nurture a growing intimacy with the Lord Jesus Christ?*

What This Intimacy Looks Like
A London newspaper published a write-in contest. The question for readers to solve was "What is the shortest way to travel to London?" Readers offered an assortment of motor routes. Some suggested train

connections. The answer that won the prize was: "The shortest way to London is with a friend."

Jesus meets you at your altar as a friend. "I no longer call you servants, because a master doesn't confide in his servants," he said. "Now you are my friends, since I have told you everything the Father told me" (John 15:15). Mabel Kearns traveled with Jesus as her friend through life. Godliness is authentic living, and knowing Jesus is bona fide eternal life: "This is life eternal, that they might know thee, the only true God, and Jesus Christ, whom thou hast sent" (John 17:3, KJV).

> Cicero wisely said, "Friendship is the only thing in the world concerning the usefulness of which all mankind are in agreement."

Do you know Jesus? If so, then you have eternal life. What wonder there is in a knowing that brings with it immortality! In this information age, we often have knowledge that has no perceptible influence upon our lives. We're inundated with news from which we attempt to sort volumes of trivia from the minutia of significance. Such knowing has little impact on living. But in a prayer offered on the night of his betrayal, Jesus spoke of a knowledge that is inseparable from living (John 17:20–24). To know Jesus is to have eternal life. That is the ultimate knowledge.

Did you ever not know somebody you should have known, a former neighbor or high school buddy? That offers a moment of embarrassment, nothing worse. When flustered, my mother would call me by my brother Bob's name, then my sister Judy's. I would hold my breath and hope she didn't call me Taffy, the dog, before she thought of Dan. It's possible to know someone well and misspeak his or her name. And it's possible to think you know someone when you scarcely know him or her at all.

An introduction to another person entitles us to claim we know her: "Do you know Freida?"

"Yes, I met her at a friend's home last year."

That kind of knowledge has little significance. It's not connected to anything vital. If we lost it, life would not be impaired. We must recognize that kind of knowledge for what it is and lay it aside if we want to know Christ and possess eternal life.

For a man to know his wife is to know her thoughts and feelings, her moods and inclinations, her desires and responses, her joys and sorrows. For instance, Nancy and I have a house full of antiques, or "old stuff," as most might call it. On a business trip, I'll often visit an antique store and look for a piece of glassware for Nancy. I can pick up an item, declare, "Nancy will appreciate this," and occasionally be right, because I know her. Yet after thirty years of marriage, she still surprises me. Nancy continues to grow, and there are mysteries about her I haven't yet discovered.

Do you know Jesus—personally, intimately, as a friend? Be careful with your answer. Judas Iscariot traveled with Jesus for three years, and the best he could have said was, "I thought I knew him, but I didn't know him at all." Judas did not have the knowledge of Jesus that brings with it eternal life.

I promise, with God's help, to nurture a growing intimacy with the Lord Jesus Christ. To help us nurture this relationship, let's learn from someone who knew Jesus well. The apostle John was the "beloved disciple," part of an inner circle that knew Jesus "up close and personal." No one, except possibly Mary, knew Jesus better than John, who counseled, "We know that we have come to know him if we obey his commands. The man who says 'I know him,' but does not do what he says is a liar" (1 John 2:3–4, NIV).

Now, how many people boast that they know Jesus? Those are strong words. There can be no knowledge of Jesus without obedience. If we aren't doing what Jesus tells us to do, we do not know him. The apostle John was such a gentleman that it strikes me as odd that he would call someone a liar. I have a friend who is so unflappable that he handles every situation with grace and ease. The other day, when he became indignant over an injustice, raised his voice, and shook his finger, I sat chuckling with approval. It was so out of character, I didn't know he had it in him to get riled up. Jesus called John a "son of thunder" (Mark 3:17), so apparently others had met his boiling point. In Scripture, however, we rarely find John upset.

But here is one thing that made his blood boil: A person who claimed he knew Jesus but wasn't living as Jesus taught. John's voice would rise, his finger would wag, and he would look that person in the eye and unequivocally declare, "You're a liar. You don't know Jesus. If you knew him, you'd conduct yourself differently; you'd live as he taught us to live."

Obedience is essential. My nephew Joe is an oarsman for the University of Michigan rowing team. Joe doesn't stroke the oar when he feels like it or at the speed he chooses. He submits to the will of the lead strokesman. Joe has but one will as an oarsman, and that is the will of the leader.

Here's another issue that raised the thunder in John: "He that loveth not, knoweth not God" (1 John 4:18, KJV). A person will always become like his or her god.

There are places on this globe where millions of people worship millions of gods. These gods or spirits have differing moods and levels of evil. Time and expense are given to appeasing gods who are users, abusers, and even killers. On multiple occasions, I've witnessed the casting out of possessive spirits or demons that were destructive killers. Yet for centuries, the temple priests of these gods have kept young girls enslaved as temple prostitutes. People become like their gods, even when their gods are users and abusers.

> *People become like their gods, even when their gods are users and abusers.*

On other parts of this planet, there are millions of people who worship a god who is not known for love and mercy. Their god is exacting, demanding, and heartlessly vengeful. With these people, the murder of apostates is considered an ethical good, even when that person is your son or daughter.

In Pakistan, a Christian teenage girl led a girlfriend to faith in Jesus. The convert was put to death by her family, and the first girl was sent to prison. After seven months of an incarceration that included rape, beating, and torture, a judge released this young girl. Shortly afterward the judge was murdered. These things happen because people become like the god they worship.

The gospel writer Mark wrote of Jesus and another acquaintance, "Jesus felt genuine love for this man as he looked at him" (Mark 10:21). One might guess he was referring to Peter or Andrew. But the reference is to the rich young ruler who eagerly asked Jesus, "What shall I do to get eternal life?" (verse 17). Jesus told him to loosen his ties to material possessions and follow him. The young man's "face fell, and he went sadly away" (verse 22). The rich young ruler measured the price of following Jesus and decided it was too costly. What god had he become like?

Did you notice that Jesus loved this man even as he walked away? He did not withdraw his love when the young man turned his back on him. This was a man who walked out of Jesus' life, and yet Jesus loved him still. How opposite that is from killing those who turn their backs on ruthless gods!

John hit the bull's eye when he asserted, "He that loveth not, knoweth not God." The God of creation, of Hebrew history, of Scripture, of Jesus Christ and the apostles, is the God of love, who gave his only Son to die for our sins. To know Christ is to be like him.

Through one of her relatives, I learned that Mabel Kearns had been wounded in marriage. Mabel never spoke of this, never complained or soiled her husband's memory, nor anyone else's. We become like the God we know.

After fourteen years of imprisonment in communist Romania, Richard Wurmbrand met Borila, who boasted how he volunteered to exterminate Jews in Transmistra, killing hundreds with his own hands. Mr. Wurmbrand tells the story of how he invited the man to his home as a guest to enjoy Ukrainian music. Midway through the evening, Wurmbrand turned to Borila and said:

"If you look through that curtain you can see someone is asleep in the next room. It's my wife, Sabina. Her parents, her sisters and her twelve-year-old brother have been killed with the rest of the family. You told me that you had killed hundreds of Jews near Golta, and that is where they were taken. . . . We can assume that you are the murderer of her family. . . . Now— let's try an experiment. I shall wake my wife and tell her who you are, and what you have done. I can tell you what will happen. My wife will not speak one word of reproach! She'll embrace you as if you were her brother. She'll bring you supper, the best things she has in the house."[1]

Then Richard offered Borila the challenging truth at the core of his "experiment." He said, "If Sabina, who is a sinner like us all, can forgive and love like this, imagine how Jesus, who is perfect Love, can forgive and love you!"

Wurmbrand tells how Borila melted before the love of God, fell to his knees, and cried out to the Lord. Richard Wurmbrand then woke Sabina, told her the story, and brought her out. He reports:

She came out in her dressing-gown and put out her arms to embrace him: then both began to weep and to kiss each other again and again. I have never seen bride and bridegroom kiss with such love and passion and purity as this murderer and the survivor among his victims. Then, as I foretold, Sabina went to the kitchen to bring him food.[2]

Richard could anticipate how Sabina would act because he knew her so well. And he could predict that she would love and forgive like Jesus, because he knew that Sabina knew Jesus intimately.

Those who know Jesus become like him in heart and conduct. So if you want to be a person of promise, join me in saying, *I promise, with God's help, to nurture a growing intimacy with the Lord Jesus Christ.*

Intimacy Leads to Worship

The old axiom says, "Familiarity breeds contempt." In other words, the longer we know people, the more we know their character flaws, temperamental weaknesses, and generally annoying eccentricities. Those who know me well could fill volumes with my faults and idiosyncrasies. Surely many such lists already exist in the memories and journals of my cohorts!

However, when it comes to Christ, familiarity breeds worship. If you don't worship the Lord, you don't know him. Wake up, strangers to Jesus: Life is short. To know him is to possess life eternal and a worshiping heart.

Worship is easy—as easy as going out on a date with the person you want to be with more than anyone else in the world. Pretending to worship is hard. It's like going out on a sympathy date with a bore who makes you cringe with every sentence.

Mabel Kearns had a worship date every morning in her trailer. And when our church was started, she had a special worship date every Sunday morning.

How beautiful are the parallels:

• Lovers give gifts of affection. Worshipers give offerings to the Lord.
• Lovers compliment the one adored. Worshipers sing the praises of Jesus and speak highly of him at

every opportunity.

• Lovers who are separated for a while anticipate the mail and reread every letter two or three times. Worshipers waiting for the return of Jesus pore over his Word with delight.

• Lovers sit alone, remembering and savoring the sweet words spoken at the last encounter. Worshipers meditate on Christ's love and promises in the quiet moments of life.

• Lovers kiss each other. Worshipers "kiss the son" in adoration (Psalm 2:12, KJV).

In love and worship, the heart becomes tender in the healthiest way (Psalm 95:8). When one mocks God and nothing harmful seems to happen, the heart becomes hardened and ignoring him becomes easier. When prayer life diminishes and no disaster results, the heart hardens itself into a prayerless life. Non-worship hardens the heart. It is the worshiper of the Lord Jesus Christ who maintains a tender heart that is aware of him. The one who sings "Amazing Grace" will experience amazing grace. The one who hums "Thank You, Lord" is the one whose heart remains grateful.

> *Worshipers, like lovers, please each other. In worship we please our Lord, whose pleasure, in turn, delights us.*

Worshipers, like lovers, please each other. So we can be sure that God is delighted with our worship. Don Worch, director of a children's home in Indiana, spoke at a church family-life conference I attended. The first night he left us with this teaser to bring us back: "What does every child want most in life? Tomorrow night I'll give the answer." Twenty-four hours later we learned, "What every child wants most is to please Mom and Dad." God is our Father and Jesus is our Savior. We want to please them. In worship we please our Lord, whose pleasure, in turn, delights us.

Worshipers know Jesus with an intimacy that non-worshipers never know. The Lord said of a generation of non-worshipers, "They have not known my ways" (Psalm 95:10, KJV). Non-worshipers may know *about* the Lord. But worshipers know the Lord *himself.* As lovers know their beloved in ways no others do, so God reveals himself—his grace, and even his Word—in special ways to those who worship him. The heart is at rest in love and worship (Psalm 95:11). The word *love* is free: it floats, it soars, it sings and dances. Those who worship Jesus know what it is to be free, to sing, to be at perfect peace.

Loveless and non-worshiping hearts are to be pitied in their restlessness. What a prize they forfeit! Non-worship is stressful to the soul. In 1956, when 62 percent of Americans were active in public worship, families and societal neighborhoods were strong. With today's decline in worship has come a rise in brokenness and heartache.

Make a Date
I promise, with God's help, to nurture a growing intimacy with the Lord Jesus Christ. Will you plan to worship Jesus outside of church once this week and again next week? Mabel spent two hours a day in worship, but she was both retired and experienced. Think of it this way: The average person spends 24 hours a week in front of the television. Certainly you can find 15 minutes a week to worship Jesus. Make a date. Tell him, "This Friday (or another day), I want to spend time worshiping you."

Make it a special occasion. Choose a place of beauty—a prairie path, a park, or the sunniest corner of your home. Carry your Bible on this worship date to read about God's love. Think of two or three things you are truly thankful for and tell Christ how pleased you are with his care over your life. You might sing a favorite hymn or worship chorus. You could even bring your checkbook; an act of worship may be giving an extra gift to a charitable cause or a needy person.

If worship becomes a lifestyle, your life will take on the characteristics and aura of Jesus Christ. Replace spiritual compromise with the resolve, *I promise, with God's help, to nurture a growing intimacy with the Lord Jesus Christ.* Then the apostle John will look at you and say, "There is one who knows Jesus. The life and heart reveal the likeness."

That's a promise worth keeping by a person of promise.

━━━━━━━━━━━━━━━━━━━━━━━━━━━━

"Christianity stands apart from other religions for one major reason. It claims to speak for a God who personally seeks an intimate relationship with human beings and spares no expense to make it possible."
—*Sandra Wilson*, Into Abba's Arms

"It takes time to know Christ intimately. He has no favorites, but he does have intimates."
—*Vance Havner*

I've tried in vain a thousand ways
My fears to quell, my hopes to raise;
But what I need, the Bible says
    Is ever, only Jesus.

15

My soul is night, my heart is steel,
I cannot see, I cannot feel;
For light and life I must appeal
   In simple faith to Jesus. . . .
Though some should sneer, and some should blame,
I'll go with all my guilt and shame,
I'll go to Him because His name,
   Above all names is Jesus.
—*Author unknown*

CHAPTER 2

Authenticity Through Imprinting

With God's help, I promise to cultivate vital friendships that encourage me to keep my promises.

Running across the prairie in a baggy, birdlike costume, he was chased by a flock of days-old Sarus Cranes, scrambling for all they were worth. It's not easy following a grownup human if you're a hatchling hustling on wobbly sticklike legs. Even a bird is an unmistakable toddler at that stage. The scientist, dressed like a mascot for a junior high football game, demonstrated an experiment in rearing birds. (If science had looked this fun when I was in school, maybe I would have opted for a career in biology.)

The International Crane Foundation of Baraboo, Wisconsin, is leading the world in saving the crane population from extinction. A trip to Baraboo will introduce you to every crane species found on this globe. Viewing the outdoor, zoolike displays, you'll *ooh* and *aah* at the White-naped Crane, the African Hooded Crane, the Siberian Crane, the Chinese Black-necked Crane, the Asia Sarus Crane, and, of course, the Whooping Crane.

What you won't see is Crane City, that portion of the ICF compound visitors are never permitted to enter. The birds housed there are protected from any visual contact with human beings. Orphaned birds are fed by humans dressed in silly crane outfits with beaks extending from the right hand—I mean, wing. Apparently misplaced beaks don't bother these crane chicks, as long as they are fed. Crane City birds will be taught to run and fight and fly by humans in these crane costumes. Later, these birds will be introduced to other cranes in the wild and hopefully will survive to propagate the species.

The cranes visitors are permitted to observe serve as breeders, egg layers. But there is no hope of them functioning in the wild, because they have been imprinted through human contact. These cranes relate to humans, sometimes in human ways. Even those that aggressively prepare to attack you have been too imprinted by human sight and care to survive without human provision. "One of the main problems with hand-reared chicks is that they become imprinted on human caretakers: they orient to humans instead of cranes as their species and, consequently, show no fear of people. This confusion could lead to the death of an introduced crane because cranes are hunted in many areas of the world."[1]

> Cranes aren't the only creatures being imprinted by others for their good or detriment. You and I are being imprinted.

These cranes are considered inauthentic. In a picture they appear genuine, but inside their hearts and heads, they are compromised and have become less than cranes.

Crane City birds are sequestered from human imprint. What little human exposure they do experience is through contact with scientists outfitted and taught to act like cranes. Why? *Because authentic cranes are those that receive authentic crane imprinting.*

Cranes aren't the only creatures being imprinted by others for their good or detriment. You and I are being imprinted. Our children are being imprinted. Society is undergoing a national and international imprinting. Children of God who aren't imprinted by godly men and women of the Christian species struggle for identity and survival. There is a spiritual panic in the hearts of many in this culture who seek a believable imprint: Who am I? What does life mean? What is my sexuality? What does it mean to be a man, or a woman, or just plain human? What's most important in my life? Credible imprinting is essential. I hear the cry of bewildered lives looking for hope and value in life.

Authentic, fully functioning Christians are those God's Spirit imprints through other healthy Christians who have wisdom and virtue to share. This has been the pattern since Christ imprinted the twelve who followed him, since Peter and John strengthened each other as they launched the Jerusalem church (Acts 3—4).

Where Imprinting Comes From

I'm grateful for both the imprinting I received and didn't receive as a child. Our home didn't have a television until my seventeenth year in 1962, when a relative died. The rest of the family conspired, "Herm and Doris Lupton may be the last family in the state without a TV. Our departed's television goes into their house." The picture tube burned out a month later, but I never asked to have it repaired. As a high school senior, I found it easier to tell friends, "Our television's broken" than "We don't have a TV yet." Life was too full as it was. Where would I find time to sit and stare?

There are only a few of us left who were raised without childhood television imprinting. But the experience convinces me that we would do well to minimize media imprinting and maximize positive, person-to-person imprinting.

Ninety-nine percent of my imprinting came through teachers, books, church, and friends. From among my teachers, I attempted to choose whom I would allow to imprint my life. I may be a bit deluded in alleging to have pulled this off, but it was a game I consciously played. The story of captive students Shadrach, Meshach, and Abednego and their resistance to inappropriate imprinting in Babylon excited me (Daniel 1:3ff). There were teachers of whom I was skeptical, and I tried to minimize the impression they were making on me. Other teachers gained my confidence and my attention.

Books are imprinting tools. As a fifth-grader I operated a popular lending library for boys at Woodville School. Each day, fellow students checked out Hardy Boys titles and returned the books after they'd read them. Soon, however, I upgraded to *Youth on the March* by Billy Graham, *Foxe's Book of Christian Martyrs*, and missionary books by Jonathan Goforth. These left an imprint on my life that endures to this day.

My church permanently imprinted my life—for the good. I weep for those I know who have been adversely imprinted through church-related episodes. As hard as I try, I can't think of a day, person, or happening that I'm angry about in my church background. The churches I grew up in were full of wonderful people and glorious events that I enjoy reliving in my memories.

Teachers, books, and churches are all related to people. A book is a story or account told by a person. A church is a gathering of people. Teachers are wonderfully special people, in spite of what you may hear from your children! The imprints on my life have come from people, most of whom I chose and a few who were imposed on me.

A Mentor's Imprint

My most influential and indelible imprinting came from those people chosen as friends and mentors. My early mentoring friends were many, though mentor wasn't in my vocabulary thirty years ago. Mentors, like springtime and Thanksgiving Day, are savory highlights in my life. I chose my vital imprinting friendships, and I give God the glory for placing wonderful mentors in my teen years. Later, I became deliberate in mentor selection, and I recommend that practice to you.

Dr. Howard Hendricks suggests that each of us seek to have three levels of imprinting friends in our lives: "You need a Paul. You need a Barnabas. And you need a Timothy."[2] If you're a woman, please don't be put off by these male names. Female relationships, like older Elizabeth and younger Mary or the women who supported each other at the crucifixion of Christ, are equally significant, though less prominent in the Bible. Perhaps the less frequent highlighting of female models is because women tend to be better at setting their own examples.

The mentor Hendricks refers to is the apostle Paul of the New Testament who mentored or imprinted many young Christians with his wisdom and experience. The Pauls in your life are those older people who will be open and honest with you, sharing their observations about your life while being transparent with their own stories, successes, and disappointments. Your Timothys are the younger ones, in age or Christian experience, whom Christ allows you to disciple and imprint. Finally, Barnabas friends are spiritual peers, friends, colleagues, and buddies with whom you bond in mutual love, support, and accountability.

Surveys show that while men tend to be lacking in Barnabas relationships, women are more adept at becoming intimate friends with one another. The other two relationships—the Paul and Timothy types—are largely absent in today's North American society. These are desperately needed if we are to be positively imprinted Christian men and women. That's why I'm urging you to join me in saying, *With God's help, I promise to cultivate vital friendships that encourage me to keep my promises.*

Level One Vital Friendships: Paul
God designed each crane to learn from its elder cranes, from hatching through each stage of development. The wrong kind of imprinting, such as that from a human, leaves the young crane's identity confused. Since crane psychiatrists don't exist, the confused crane requires a lifetime of institutional care. A lack of quality imprinting at migration season leaves a crane sitting out in the cold. The bird doesn't know which path to take any more than a thirteen-year-old girl without a righteous imprint from an older woman knows which path to follow.

If I were a teenager or a new follower of Christ, I wouldn't let mentoring friendships just happen or not happen. I'd purposefully find mentors, what Pat McManus calls the "old men" of life. Pat's father died when he was only eight, leaving him without significant male imprinting. Growing up in northern Idaho, Pat longed more than anything to be a woodsman, an outdoorsman, or even a rugged mountain man. Pat is a humorist, but the collecting of old men has an underlying urgency in his literature.

He writes, "When I was a youngster, grit was the chief remedy for a variety of ailments. 'What that boy needs,' an old man would prescribe, 'is more grit.' A deficiency in grit was considered more serious than a shortage of Vitamin B. Grit, I've learned over the years, is one of the best things an old man has to offer a kid."[3]

Nancy's life shows plenty of grit—as in staying married to me for three decades. Much of her Christian grit came from the Lewis farm. Nancy accepted Christ as Savior through the invitation of her high school friend Suzie Lewis. After that, Nancy spent many a Saturday night sleepover at the farm, and went to church with the Lewis family the next morning. Suzie's mom, Ruth, was a Paul, or should I say an *Elizabeth*, to Nancy. Ruth was a model and mentor in seeing God's hand for good even when the crops were thin. Ruth showed how to be a faithful wife helping with the harvest, even driving a tractor when husband Dean had a bad back. Ruth sang her way through the day, showing how to integrate work and worship. And Ruth always had a smile and an encouraging word, teaching Nancy the joy of the Lord. That adds up to a lot of grit.

> *Do you have a Paul in your life—an older man or woman—to give you the wisdom you need?*

Do you have a Paul in your life—an older man or woman—to give you the wisdom you need? Through Pat McManus, the term *old man* has become one of high honor, so please understand it that way. When I was a young fellow wet behind the ears, the old men of my life were generally younger than I am now. At fifteen, some of the "old men" in my life weren't out of their twenties. Others were in their retirement years.

Timothy's "old man" was Paul, who in mentoring him said, "Don't let anyone think less of you because you are young" (1 Timothy 4:12). Young professionals often have a credibility gap with the older generation. Paul's advice was to not let that be a cop-out for ineffectiveness. "Be an example to all believers in what you teach, in the way you live, in your love, your faith, and your purity," he said. We always can make excuses for ourselves: too young, too old, or lack the right education. The mentor you need is the one who won't let you get away with a pity party about how tough life is, how unfairly you are treated, and how you therefore don't have to measure up. A good mentor will make you stand up, shape up, and step out.

The old man or woman in your life will not hesitate to tell you, "Throw yourself into your tasks so that everyone will see your progress" (1 Timothy 4:15). This is what the old men in Pat's life called "grit." Work hard, do your best, and never quit or make excuses.

Warren Bolthouse was one of the old men who imprinted my life. Warren was my Youth for Christ director during high school. In his upper thirties then, Warren seemed pretty ripe to a fifteen-year-old like me. He taught me what Paul taught Timothy—to attempt big things for God, look for creative ways to share the gospel, get a Christian education, value all God's people regardless of which church they belonged to, and stand up for what's right even if it brings criticism. He taught me how to initiate a project, see a task through to completion, and clean up after an event was over. Warren taught me to stretch beyond the possible, because what's easily reachable doesn't require God or faith.

Through the years I've collected other old men to mentor me: Robert Stansfield, Wilbur Powell, Ira Ransom, Lloyd Johnson, Charles Svoboda. It's surprising how many of these don't look so old anymore. *Collected* is the right word, too. The old men or women friends of your life may or may not know they are your mentors. I've invested as many hours in each of the above mentors as they have in me, yet some may only learn of their mentoring role by reading this.

How do you begin an old man or woman relationship? Try saying, "I'd be honored if I could take you out for lunch next week. I've got a question I'd like your input on. How about Tuesday noon?" Do that once, and you'll receive good advice. Do it two or three times, and you'll have a mentoring friend, regardless of whether the word *mentor* comes up.

> *"I have a lot of respect for you. That's why I ask questions from time to time. Thanks for being a model and mentor to me."*

If I were a teenage Christian, I'd look for a youth leader or pastor for a mentor friend, plus the parents of some of my teen friends. If a single or divorced parent were raising me, I'd be bold and tell two or three adults, "I have a lot of respect for you. That's why I ask questions from time to time. Thanks for being a model and mentor to me."

My mentoring friends have taught me everything from affirming my wife's gifts and dreams to never stepping into a motel room with a woman during my travels. Through them I've learned which battles to fight and which to ignore; how God exalts the humble and humbles the proud; and when to work to support my family and when to forget work to support my family, too! They've taught me how to solve problems and avoid their mistakes. Some principles they *taught* and others I just *caught* by watching and listening. I can look back upon my life and note person after person who has served in the role of Paul to me. And I honor these relationships that have made invaluable imprints upon my life.

Level Two Vital Friendships: Timothy

Howard Hendricks suggests that another vital friendship is a Timothy. Paul needed to mentor Timothy as much as Timothy needed Paul as his "old man."

When you have a Timothy in your life, you will understand how Paul emotionally connected with Timothy as "my true child in the faith" (1 Timothy 1:2).

It's time for women and men of Christian maturity to be active rather than passive in the mentor role. My mother was a wonderful example of one who had many Timothy relationships.

Not too long ago I had this phone conversation: "Hello, I'm Dan Lupton, and I'm scheduling a conference for church leaders in your city." I was looking for direction in selecting a conference site, but the church secretary had another agenda.

"Your name is Lupton? Do you know any of the Luptons from Jackson, Michigan?"

"I was raised in Jackson, and we were the only Luptons there. If you know a Jackson Lupton, you know my family."

"How are you related to Doris Lupton?"

This conversation piqued my curiosity. "She was my mother. Why do you ask?"

"I was a college student in Jackson and attended your church. During a difficult period with a broken romance and bewilderment over many issues, your mother took me under her wing, listened to my story, counseled me, prayed for me, and in many ways mentored me. Doris was my surrogate mom for a couple of years. Today I'm married and have a good life, and I owe much of it to your mother's love and wisdom."

I'd never heard this story. Mom was a friend to many young women and didn't talk about them. She wasn't a pastor or a trained full-time professional Christian. My mother worked in a medical office all her life. But she had lived through hard times, sinful and painful years, before coming to faith in Christ. You couldn't surprise or shock her. And you could not drain her of love. She needed these younger women friends like an actor needs a stage, like a gardener needs a patch of ground.

For fifty years, the late Harry Caray was America's most recognizable baseball voice. He was the only broadcaster who could make an hour rain delay entertaining. While appearing to be a bumbling amateur for 60 years, Harry actually was a beguiling master of his craft. And he spent the last 30 years of his life training younger broadcasters. At his death, dozens of sportscasters lined up to praise Harry for the private lessons he gave them. Teaching his broadcasting secrets was a delight, a life validation, for Harry Caray.

How much more wonderful it is for Christians to place their faith imprint on younger lives. A young pastor approached me: "When Dr. David Howard of the World Evangelical Fellowship returned from Singapore, he chose a small church to join, a church with a young pastor he could help. Dan, I'm looking for someone like this, and I hope it will be you." With twenty years of pastoral experience, I saw this as God's opportunity to imprint another with the wisdom I had learned. I needed to have this Timothy as much as he needed me for his old man. That conversation was three years ago, and the relationship is only now reaching its most significant fulfillment.

When my son Larry graduated from college and accepted his first career job, he was given a desk, a computer, and a mentor. During the first 12 to 18 months of employment, his training was with one primary mentor and a few shared mentors. How much more important it is in the Christian and church world for novices, for young believers, to have mentors! Few churches achieve this as systematically as Larry's employer. So, until mentoring becomes a standard and accepted equipping ministry, it's up to you and me to accept the mentoring challenge personally.

> *Do you teach a Sunday school class or serve in a youth club? Go beyond showing up and putting in your time. Pour your life into their lives.*

Do you teach a Sunday school class or serve in a youth club? Go beyond showing up and putting in your time. Love those God has entrusted to you. Pour your life into their lives. Be their Paul, and let them be your Timothy. Mentor them. Imprint their lives, and help the new generation become strong.

Ultimate Lifetime Vital Friendships: Barnabas

Barnabas was Paul's friend and traveling companion for several years. It was Barnabas who went to Tarsus to find Saul (later the apostle Paul) and bring him to Antioch. Barnabas was the first to see Saul's potential and help it to blossom. For at least a year, Paul and Barnabas taught tag-team style in front of great numbers of people (Acts 11:25–26). This relationship was one of mutual support between equals.

It was also an honest relationship of accountability. Barnabas didn't hesitate to express disagreement and even disapproval of Paul when he thought him on the wrong side of a decision or action. When Paul lost confidence in young John Mark, Barnabas knew it was too early to quit on him and stood toe-to-toe with Paul over this issue. Paul later came to Barnabas's position that Mark was of great value to their cause (2 Timothy 4:11). Indeed! The Holy Spirit guided Mark in writing the second New Testament account of Jesus' life.

The young crane needs an "old man" crane for a true crane imprint. The adult crane needs a young crane to mentor. And all through the crane's life, it needs crane comrades for mutual imprint and support. The International Crane Foundation reports that every migration season the cranes renew the imprinting process of identification, direction, and support. They learn to stick together, to keep the flock on the right path, and to take turns cutting through the wind as "point crane" at the head of the flying *V*.

There is a season in life to have a mentor and a season to be a guiding friend. But it is always "in season" to have vital mutual friendships with Barnabas types who will remind you of your Christian identity, encourage you to stick to the right path in difficult times, and, if necessary, to fly "point" in assisting you on life's journey. "Never abandon a friend—either yours or your father's. Then in the time of need, you won't have to ask your relatives for assistance" (Proverbs 27:10).

Who was the first man to fly solo across the Atlantic? Charles Lindbergh. Who was the first woman to achieve this feat? Amelia Earhart. Who were the members of the first team to fly across an ocean? This answer might be found in an almanac, but in our western tradition, it isn't significant. Clint Eastwood and John Wayne made movie careers playing solo rugged characters. We North Americans make heroes of individuals instead of vital team relationships.

There was a period in American history when brotherhood and connectedness was the valued way of life. During the colonial era, men and women viewed their Christian experience, even their salvation, through the church community. The Mayflower Compact was a promise to not hit the shore with each person running to do his or her own thing: "We . . . Do . . . solemnly and mutually in the Presence of God and one another, covenant and combine ourselves together . . . for the general Good of the Colony; unto which we promise all due Submission and Obedience."[4] Written and signed in 1620, this pact expressed the value of mutual relationships. Musketeer style, it was "all for one, and one for all."

> *We North Americans make heroes of individuals instead of vital team relationships.*

The current societal trend is "cocooning," the practice of living within the house yet apart from others. In-the-home gyms allow people to avoid parks and sports centers. Big screen televisions and video rentals replace going out to a movie. Faxing or e-mailing your grocery order for delivery means never stepping into a market. We are learning how to live not only without committed friendships but with minimal human contact. Many homes are set up for sub-cocoons with a TV in every room. A four-member family can spend an evening entertained in four separate cocoons.

Why do we believers swing with society's pendulum? If we could make it as rugged Christian individuals, why are we given scores of "one-another" commands in Scripture?

"A new commandment I give you: *Love one another.* As I have loved you, so you must love one another" (John 13:34, NIV, italics added). Jesus calls for us to emulate him in the "one anothers" of vital friendships. Jesus wept at the tomb of Lazarus, whom he *loved.* The disciple John is described as someone Jesus *loved.* On the eve of his crucifixion Jesus declared that he *loved* his disciples as his own Father loved him. One writer's summary is that "love is the infrastructure of everything and anything worthwhile." I once heard that most people do not have five lifelong vital friendships. That seemed preposterous at the time. The question to ask is, "Are there five friends who know I love them? Are there five friends who love me enough to risk being honest with me?"

"*Be kind and compassionate to one another, forgiving each other,* just as Christ forgave you" (Ephesians 4:32, NIV, italics added). Jesus never quit on anyone. He always gave people another chance. He kept on believing in his friends. I've noticed through the years that the people I forgive the most are the people I love the most and usually the ones I enjoy the most. I have to forgive them because, like me, they speak up, offend people, make bad decisions, and fail often. I'm attracted to them because they are transparent, speak honestly, dream big dreams, attempt that which is beyond them, and take risks.

Whatever draws you to a friend has its upside and downside. To enjoy the upside, you will find yourself continually forgiving the downside. This forgiveness is an expression and proof of friendship.

"I myself am convinced, my brothers, that you yourselves are full of goodness, complete in knowledge and competent to *instruct one another*" (Romans 15:14, NIV, italics added). You know more than you suspect, and this knowledge can be valuable to your friends. If you read your Bible daily, fellowship in a healthy church, live a 24/7 Christian life, and see God minister to you and through you, you are a walking source of wisdom to friends. What you lack is enough wisdom and knowledge to adequately live your own life. That is why vital Christian friends are indispensable throughout life.

> *You know more than you suspect, and this knowledge can be valuable to your friends.*

I've given counsel to many on family, marriage, and parenting issues. So it follows that I should have the answers to all my own needs. However, it doesn't work that way because I'm emotionally wrapped up in all my personal problems. Through the years I've welcomed the instruction of friends on the same issues about which I've instructed others. It's an old axiom that "he who has himself for a lawyer has a fool for a lawyer." You may know the law as well as the attorney you hire to handle your case. But the lawyer can look at your problem from outside your box. That is the genius role of friends instructing one another. They will appraise your situation in ways you never can. You must have friends who can instruct you.

Even when you don't have a specific problem, you need to meet regularly with a few friends for fellowship and encouragement. *"Let us encourage one another"* (Hebrews 10:25, NIV, italics added).

Encouragement should be a constant flow, not a ministry reserved for times when you feel depressed. You need a friend to encourage you in keeping the promises in this book. You need a friend who will ask, "How was Jesus good to you this week?" and "What in God's Word excited you today?" You need a friend who will confidentially hold you accountable as you move toward victory over sin and the establishment of new deportment: "So, what have you done this week to show love to your children? Tell me about it." Do you have five friends you encourage in Christian experience and personal growth? This is the godly imprinting process, to motivate others in healthy spiritual habits until Jesus comes.

"Serve one another in love" (Galatians 5:13, NIV, italics added). John is a friend who lives in another country much of the time. In a phone conversation a few years ago, I told him he could stay with us any time he needed. A week later he called back to ask if I meant it. Assured that the welcome mat was always out for him, he asked, "Can you pick me up tomorrow night at O'Hare Airport?" He stayed for two weeks of personal rest and relaxation.

Another time he was deathly ill overseas, and his doctor advised him to leave that country. He became our treasured guest, and we were honored to nourish him back to health. Honor is a part of service. *"Honor one another above yourselves"* (Romans 12:10, NIV, italics added). John still asks if he is imposing or overstaying. I think it is a courtesy question, because he knows Nancy and I consider it a privilege to serve him in whatever need God permits to enter his life. Are there those you serve with honor, or who count it a joy to serve you? John and I see each other infrequently, but I also have friends I meet with weekly for prayer and advice, friends who would drop almost anything to serve me.

These vital friendships must be arranged and tended with special care. Seven years ago, David Mains phoned: "Dan, I need a prayer partner in my life, and he needs to have a concern for revival. Would you be interested in meeting Saturday mornings for mutual support and prayer for revival?" Seven years later we still meet at 7:30 A.M. each Saturday, but a phone invitation was required to upgrade casual acquaintance into vital friendship.

That's what I want you to do. Make that phone call. Come out of spiritual isolation. You may find your friendships within a church small group or covenant group. Many churches have Sunday school classes whose core members have bonded together through the years. Start talking with *someone* about spiritual things. At least touch base once every few weeks for a "spiritual checkup." But try to go well beyond that, to become a vital friend.

God created cranes, and he created you. We share this much in common with our feathered friends: Our lives are constantly being imprinted. We can either compromise the process and accept imprinting by whatever and whoever we happen to be around, or we can be purposeful and deliberate in choosing imprinting models.

At fifty-one years of age, I still have mentors—my Pauls, or old men, as Pat McManus calls them—to whom I look for imprinting. I've been entrusted with a few Timothys who look to me as their "old man." Mostly, however, it's the Barnabas friendships that I'm committed to nurturing as long as God gives me breath.

My mother has been with the Lord for eight years, yet on her birthday her lifetime "Barnabas," Jayne Ahlstrom, still calls me to say thank you for my mother's friendship. "She was always there for me, my prayer partner, encourager, and friend." Above wealth or power, seek to be remembered as a friend.

With God's help, I promise to cultivate vital friendships that encourage me to keep my promises. That's a promise worth keeping by a person of promise.

"Connecting is a kind of relating that happens when the powerful life of Christ in one person meets the good life of Christ in another. What every Christian can pour into another is the powerful passion of acceptance, a passion that flows out of the center of the gospel, a passion that fills the heart of God."
—*Larry Crabb*, Connecting

"Mentoring—The process in which successful individuals go out of their way to help others establish goals and develop the skills to reach them."
—*The Mentoring Group*

"One of the great assets of being mentored by someone is learning how to receive and sometimes shape the help given to you. You must help your mentor help you."
—*Dr. Linda Phillips-Jones*

"A friend is someone who will make us do what we can when we say we can't."
—*Ralph Waldo Emerson*

There's happiness in little things,
There's joy in passing pleasure.
But friendships are, from year to year,
The best of all life's treasure.
—*Author unknown*

CHAPTER 3

Signature List

With God's help, I promise to practice purity in thought and action.

Having a grandchild offers a third chance to grow up properly. First comes your own flawed childhood, which you remember with a mixture of fondness and regret. Second are your children's wonder years, which you recall with pride and a generous dose of denial. Third are the grandchild's glory years.

Gini is nine, and dressed up she looks lovely. I won't bore you with how bright and creative and cheerful my granddaughter is. However, last year Lutheran pastor Bill Pratt of St. Paul, Minnesota, spent a night with us in our home. A few days later we shared conference-speaking chores, and it was his duty to introduce me. He said, "This is Dan Lupton, grandfather of Gini, whom I met last week. She is only eight and charmed me, served me soft drinks, kept me laughing, and played games with me. What a great hostess she was." He went on for three or four minutes telling stories about Gini and entirely overlooking his presenting partner.

It is rarer than a short sermon for others to recognize the perfections of someone else's granddaughter. True, Bill Pratt and his wife Rita raised three sons with no little girls around to charm them, and they are a few years away from their own first grandchild. But it was still a remarkable way to be introduced.

Being a granddad is more than just a lot of fun. I've lived so much history, and Gini is so little interested in it. What stories should a granddad inflict on a girl about to be assaulted by puberty? What does a young person need to know about purity in thought and action? My granddaughter shows such wonderful promise, and I don't want her to settle for some weak compromise. What should she be taught about herself and how to live her life?

I made an amazing discovery. The proverbial concepts that a young teen should hear from an elder are the same verities the elder needs as the backbone of his or her life. These principles are for any who want to live an authentic life and not be what Oklahomans call "all hat and no cattle." For city folks, that means a fool's gold cowboy—all talk and no walk. This chapter is for all of us, and it should change your life for the good forever.

I'm Special

Have you seen the poster "I'm special because God don't make no junk"? That's the beginning of purity, to picture your life as possessing unique intrinsic worth. The first line of moral defense is to know how much you count to God and others. And a poor self-image is an early alert of high moral risk.

We know of no impurities in the life of John the Baptist. From his earliest days, Johnny heard he was so special to the Lord that God's Spirit physically moved him while he was still in the womb (Luke 1:41). You would feel special, too, if at every birthday gathering you were reminded how many rejoiced at your birth: "For he will be great in the eyes of the Lord. He must never touch wine or hard liquor, and he will be filled with the Holy Spirit, even before his birth" (Luke 1:14–15). Young John might have felt like the most precious piece of china in a palace. The fact that his parents were old didn't detract from his self-image. He was special to God.

This is the beginning of purity. John, the eventual baptizer, not only saw himself as special but saw everyone he knew as special, too. He treasured his life and would not defile it with profanity, lies, or immorality. And he valued everyone else so highly that he led them to turn away from impurities and seek God's best in life.

Whether or not you feel special affects your posture: how you sit, stand, and walk. It affects what you attempt, how you love and receive love. It affects what you allow in your life and how you treat other people.

Purity in life can begin with the way people handled you as an infant, how they cared for you or neglected you. They either let you cry or they quickly responded to your call for help. From your first days, you sensed what the people around you thought about you. Purity in life is an outgrowth of whether you were complimented or criticized. America has a major problem of gang warfare and related drive-by shootings. But behind those hardened faces are young people who have rarely felt loved.

A group of Chicago radio sports jocks were discussing Mike Tyson, former heavyweight boxing champion. A convicted felony rapist, he also bit off part of boxer Evander Holyfield's ear—twice. The consensus of these grizzled Chicago sports voices was pity for Mike, because when he was growing up, no one made him feel loved or special.

God wants you to receive your self-image from him, letting that drive a life of purity. The beginning of your relationship with God is to come to him repentant, humble, often broken, sometimes shattered in guilt from all the impurity in your life. But Jesus will cleanse you, nourish you, hold you, comfort you, bless you, call you his child of love, and in every way make you feel so special, you'll know how John the Baptist felt. If you were seldom held, Jesus holds you in his hands. If you were abandoned, he will never leave you. If you were orphaned, he adopts you. If you were made to feel like a slave, he calls you a prince and a priest.

> *If you were seldom held, Jesus holds you in his hands. If you were abandoned, he will never leave you.*

Out of this comes a life of purity. We avoid the impurities associated with idolatry because we are the holy temple of God and God's treasured sons and daughters (2 Corinthians 6:14–18). We live in conformity with whom we believe we are. We never outgrow our need to battle life's impurities through our relationship with God.

Gini, you are not only special to my family, you are wonderfully special to Jesus.

And so are you, extraordinary reader. Live as though your body and soul are treasures to protect and keep clean.

Our World Is Beautiful but Fallen
There is much that I appreciate in today's culture. There is such diversity in the arts, any weekend I can find a concert or play that is enjoyable and uplifting. I have great memories of growing up in the '50s, but I wouldn't return to segregated lunch-

rooms for anything in the world. Nor would I return to typewriters and carbon paper. I benefit from today's culture, but I must also beware.

Our culture is flooded with every kind of compromise. Some of you think of impurity primarily in sexual connotations. We are inundated with sexual immorality and depravity. The hit television show *Seinfeld* was one of the typically debased. A major recurrent theme was that human sexuality was a game, a sport to be played often with a variety of participants, a form of recreation like bowling or Frisbee, never experienced in marriage, with no worse consequences than a farewell. To mock sin subtly can be as dangerous as blatant pornography.

Sitcom humor lulls us into accepting immoral values while we laugh with the children and eat popcorn. Believers of any age need to be aware that the dominant morals and values of today's culture require revival or God's judgment. Indeed, we've experienced a 30-year assault on the sanctity of sex and home. Now we're in the early harvest of a generation of broken lives. And I, a Christian in my fifties, need to remember that as a check on my own values. Whatever your decade of life, you know there is no immunity from influence of the cultural slide. Will you join me in this commitment? *I promise, with God's help, to be sexually pure in thought and action.*

But the impurity that would swamp us is more than sexual. We are also being flooded with impurity in the guise of spiritual enlightenment. The Bible says that Satan can masquerade as an angel of light (2 Corinthians 11:14). Darkness lurks. This week I received a catalog of workshops from the "Infinity Foundation for Infinite Ways of Learning." Infinite ways were offered on how to become spiritually enlightened—but Jesus Christ was never mentioned.

Workshops are offered in awakening to the spirit, energy healing, practical Buddhism, the ancient Judaic Kabbalah, mysticism, tarot card reading, journeying through the chakras, the sacred spiral of life, and more. This group performs weddings, commitment ceremonies for those who want to live together without marriage, baby blessings, house blessings, memorial remembrances, and rites of passage.

> *All that glitters is not gold, and all that is spiritual is not God. The risen Christ is the way, the truth, and the life.*

One will certainly bump into spiritual experiences through these events. But all that glitters is not gold, and all that is spiritual is not of God. The risen Christ is the way, the truth, and the life. No one comes to God except through him (John 14:6). Spiritual compromise carries eternally damning consequences, even as following Jesus promises eternal reward. So it's time to resolutely and solemnly *promise, with God's help, to be spiritually pure.*

Our culture is flooded with ethical impurity. There is a general collapse of integrity from the highest political offices to the smallest home businesses. One senses that we have a government of the rich, by the rich, and for the rich. Senator Dan Coates of Indiana declared he wouldn't run for re-election because he didn't want to spend two years raising money for the race. The time commitment is an ethical issue. Is it right to spend a third of your elected term seeking another term? The money issue is also pressing. Those that give generously to your election bid expect much in return.

"Society can function as long as 90 percent of the

people can be trusted 90 percent of the time." A high school teacher taught me that 35 years ago. It's probably the only thing I remember from his class. You and I believe that 100 percent of Christians need to be trusted 100 percent of the time.

Last week at an Italian restaurant, Nancy and I were charged for three meals when we had ordered four. I brought this to the owner's attention. He looked at me in amazement. "You're the first," he said.

"I'm the first what?" I asked.

"You're the first here to ever pay up when you were undercharged."

With a smile I replied, "I'm a Christian gentleman, and I want to please my conscience and my Savior." The next time you are undercharged or given too much change, square the deal. It's part of purity.

Temptations to compromise ethical integrity happen to each of us with unexpected regularity. From being undercharged, to falsifying an employment application, to not returning what was borrowed, Satan supplies us with ample opportunities to live an ethical lie. What should you do? Right now you should write on the blackboard of your heart: *With God's help, I resolve to be pure in all my business affairs, to cheat no one, to owe no one, to honor God in word and contract.*

Our culture is impure in its interests, its fake news broadcasts, and its ease in destroying lives with false accusations. Rumors and gossip fill up hours of television news, even when there are no facts to report. Leaks of accusations destroy reputations. The *Globe* and *The National Enquirer* peer into places that are private and titillate under the guise of journalism. A former reporter suggests, "You can spill coffee on a

43

newspaper today without much danger of wetting a fact, although you will drown a lot of quotes." Who said what about whom is big buck busybody business. And it is all impure. The lives and reputations of others should be guarded as a sacred trust. May God help me as *I promise to be pure in what I think and say about others and in what I watch and read.* I will uphold the reputations of others and bear false witness against no one.

Gini, this is an impure age. Don't accept it as normal. It hasn't always been this way. But I'm praying for a spiritual awakening that will restore a righteous culture in our land.

Impurity Demands a Heavy Tax

The unwelcome army of the Philistines had invaded Israel like weeds invade my garden, as impurity will seek to infiltrate even a Christian's life. The Philistine encroachers were pagan, profane, and relished mocking the one, true God. When a dominant sin plants itself in a Christian's life, it mocks our God and Savior—it defies us to slay it, pretends to be all-powerful, and leads to depression.

During the Philistine occupation, Saul was king of Israel, and a spirit of depression and fear possessed him. He lost the fullness and joy of the Lord's presence (1 Samuel 16:14). One writer reminds us:

> See the effects of sin upon the spirit of man. "The merry-hearted do sigh." Life loses its wing and its song. The buoyancy and the optimism die out of the soul. The days move with heavy feet, and duty becomes very stale and unwelcome. If only our ears were keen enough we should hear many a place of hollow laughter moaning with troubled and restless sighs. The soul cannot sing when God is defied. But see another effect of sin. *"The earth moaneth."* . . . Sin

44

spreads its desolation everywhere. When I sin, I become the center of demoralizing forces which influence the universe.[1]

Yesterday while traveling I listened to a few minutes of Dr. Laura Schlesinger's radio talk show. An eighteen-year-old girl called to tell how much she was in love with a military man. For weeks they spent all non-working hours together and were sexually active. This week she discovered the man is married. His wife was living in another state but would soon be moving on base. The young woman was in terrible heartache. She called the man's wife and told her about the affair. The pain spread. Friends were involved who had covered up for their buddy in uniform who was trapped in the middle of pain and shame. This story was broadcast to millions who moaned with her. The nation moans. The sound of moaning multiplies as similar stories are heard in every city, town, and countryside.

> *Each impurity, each defilement, takes a toll on a person's life. Each sin brings a bit of death.*

Dr. Laura was direct: Sex is for marriage. Sex outside of marriage brings pain. The office flirtation is a fire to consume your life. "Forsaking all others," we cleave to our spouse. Anything else will bring pain as it destroys lives. Single and married people must equally respect sexual purity.

Each impurity, each defilement, takes a toll on a person's life. Each sin brings a bit of death. One assumes, *I'll rule my life in rebellion to morals*. But sin answers, *I rule, and you die*. In sin, love dies, health dies, relationships die, energy dies, nations die, the conscience dies, hopes die, and in the end, the body dies.

Paul Harvey, on a noon broadcast, explained that he keeps a file for shamed public figures. Each time a person is convicted of a crime or publicly embarrassed, he puts that news piece in a folder. Paul reported that almost invariably such a person will have a major illness within six months. The toll of the stress of sin is invasive. Will you now commit yourself to no more sexual compromises in thought and deed?

Gini, I want you to live as a godly woman. Let no man steal your heart or body. Keep it and give it in marriage to a special man of God.

To Be Pure, One Must Reign in Life

The authentic life is a life that is in charge. The fool's gold life takes orders from lust and drugs and hate and pride and greed. What runs your life? Who reigns over your life? Do you feel controlled by others, out of control, or the master of your life?

Oh, we want to be the master of our ship! Hundreds of thousands annually begin entrepreneurial businesses, not with the expectation of riches but with the hope that they will answer to themselves and not to another. It is suffocating to feel that your life is not your own, even if you receive a substantial paycheck with it. We regularly hear from professional athletes who complain that management treats them like servants. It's hard to be sympathetic with someone receiving millions of dollars to play a game. But we do feel their pain, because we all want to be free.

Princess Diana was admired and envied worldwide. She received earned praise for her compassion on society's poor and wounded. Thousands imagined themselves in Diana's place: beautiful, rich, with palaces and power and all the pleasures of a throne. All happy daydreams except to Diana. She was a princess who couldn't rule. Her life was a pitiful cell. Her marriage was more dungeon than throne. She fled photographers like a fox fleeing the hounds. Even people with thrones can't always rule in life.

Worse yet is to feel controlled by unclean habits and impure thoughts. I read recently that there are a million web sites dedicated to pornography. Twenty thousand web sites would be an epidemic. Men, women, and youth are addicted to visiting these, to producing them, and to being seen in them. Others are addicted to lying, shoplifting, hate, gossip, and cursing. There are physical addictions to alcohol, drugs, and junk foods.

The good news—yes, "gospel" good news—is that God intends us to be free of enslaving addictions to impurity and to reign in life instead. Part of the re-demptive grace that comes from Jesus' crucifixion and resurrection is that we can once again reign in life.

From the beginning, we who were created in the image of God were designed to be free and to reign. "Male and female he created them. God blessed them and told them, 'Multiply and fill the earth and subdue it. Be masters . . .'" (Genesis 1:27–28). God intended for us to rule our environment and our lives. That is still the goal and challenge. With God's help, you can be pure in thought and action.

Adam and Eve forfeited their freedom as they ate the out-of-bounds fruit. They lost their crowns and scepters. They became exiles from their palace gar-den. Since that day, humankind has failed in all attempts to be the king or queen God intended, though the desire constantly stirs in each of us. Since that event, sin and death have ruled our passions and bodies.

But Jesus has turned the tables on sin and death. "For if one man's offense meant that men should be slaves to death all their lives, it is a far greater thing that through another man, Jesus Christ, men by their acceptance of his more than sufficient grace and righteousness should live all their lives like kings" (Romans 5:17, Phillips). Donald Grey Barnhouse adds, "God is a great transformer of lives. He turns slaves into kings. He deposes the dynasty of sin, chains it in the dungeon, and enthrones the dynasty of righteousness. He takes the child of Adam and lifts him to reign with Christ."[2]

> *Humankind has failed in all attempts to be the king or queen God intended, though the desire constantly stirs in each of us.*

It is time to dislodge and dethrone all the impurities of life and rule our lives in righteousness by the help of Jesus Christ.

Gini, with passion in my heart, I want you to know Christ and his grace so that you reign in life. I want you to live God's plan and purpose for your life, with no regrets for wasted years in sin's bondage. Let Christ make you a princess.

Lists and Purity

I can't go through a day without lists. Are you that way? For me there is the daily business to-do list. It tells me who and what I can't put off any longer. There is my honey-do list, which is filled with scores of household projects such as painting the bathroom and fixing the leaking roof. This is not always seen as an important list, but I wouldn't dare tell Nancy I didn't have it. My favorite is my want-to-do list. This list is so sensitive it isn't written down, lest a spy should see it, but I fastidiously keep it current. If I want ginger ale and popcorn, I get it and check it off my want-to-do list. I love top-ten lists and can't avoid Christmas lists, grocery lists, and bill-paying lists. Even time away requires a vacation list. How would I know if I'd had a good time if I hadn't checked off my vacation-plan list? As a child I had a chore list, if I wanted my allowance, and a Scripture memory list to win a week at church summer camp. Why, my first day in kindergarten I was sent home with a pencil-box list!

My dear wife, Nancy, put up with my rambling confession as I packed my suitcase while checking off the "things to take on a conference trip" list. She comforted me with, "Just be glad you're not a pilot going through the pre-flight check-off list. Or Jim Collins. He has the most important list, and you don't even know about it. Here, listen to this tape."

Telling a list man he doesn't know the number-one list is like telling a lexicographer she doesn't know words or a fisherman he doesn't know how to use a tape measure. I listened to the cassette.

"How many of you have a to-do list?" the co-author of *Built to Last* (29 months on *Business Week's* bestseller list) asked in a conference of church leaders at Chicago's Willowcreek Church. Most hands were raised in pride over their to-do lists. I snickered at these amateur list makers. Jim followed with, "And how many of you explicitly next to it have a stop-doing list?" Laughter captured the auditorium because no one had ever heard of a stop-doing list— including me. My head hung in humiliation. Jim continued, "After today, I hope all of you have a stop-doing list. Start a stop-doing list when you leave this room. Because what you stop doing can be as important in achieving your objectives as what you start doing."

> "What you stop doing can be as important in achieving your objectives as what you start doing."

I thought this would be easy. Giving a list man a new list was akin to giving a Hershey bar to a chocoholic. But it wasn't easy. I was venturing into new cranial territory.

To write a book, one needs a place to write, read, and pray. In my home, I've set aside a room for such purposes. The walls are lined with books. In front of a window is a desk for my computer and notes. The only chair is a straight-back wooden chair: Chair selection is important. I have nothing against overstuffed ottomans. It was an emotional moment for me last summer when Nancy threw my recliner out. After nineteen years, it was broken in and well formed, like my old slippers. (She threw those out, too.) But my writing chair is so uncomfortable that I never get drowsy. Writing and drowsiness are as incompatible as wives and old chairs.

The room was arranged for writing, except for one piece. Did you know that every Chicago Bulls game is televised? And did you know that 82 basketball games can interfere with the goal to read and write? I unplugged the television and gave it to my daughter. Writing a book requires a to-do list and a parallel stop-doing list. My first stop-doing item was: Stop keeping a TV in the writing room.

Jim Collins is paid huge amounts of money to speak and consult with businesses. What he has discovered with his not-to-do list is in reality a major Bible theme that Moses employed, Jesus taught, and the apostles preached and practiced. The achievement of goals requires a double list—a to-do list and a stop-doing list.

The famous Ten Commandments include a to-do list (love God exclusively; set aside a dedicated Sabbath; honor your father and mother) and a stop-doing list (stop worshiping anything made by humans, stop taking the name of the Lord in vain, stop killing, stop sexual immorality, stop stealing, stop lying about people, stop coveting). The goals behind those commandments are to live a pure and satisfying life as God intended, so society can function and prosper.

It seems to me that Jesus had a love-hate relationship with lists. He began his famous Sermon on the Mount with a list of nine ways poor and persecuted people could count life blessed. "God blesses those who mourn, for they will be comforted. . . . God blesses those who are merciful, for they will be shown mercy. God blesses those whose hearts are pure, for they will see God" (Matthew 5:4–8).

However, he rejected human-contrived and misused lists of rules for judging others, righteous or unrighteous. Ignoring these, he ate with forbidden people such as tax collectors and went to taboo places like Samaria. Jesus forcefully restated these stop-doing lists, coming to the heart and spirit of the issues: "You have heard that the Law of Moses says, 'Do not commit adultery.' But I say, anyone who even looks at a woman with lust in his eyes has already committed adultery with her in his heart. . . . You have heard . . . 'Love your neighbor' and hate your enemy. But I say, love your enemies!" (Matthew 5:27–28, 43–44).

The apostles were masters at the double list. The apostle Paul opens Ephesians 4 with a to-do list so beautiful it reads like poetry: "I, a prisoner for serving the Lord, beg you to lead a life worthy of your calling, for you have been called by God. Be humble and gentle. Be patient with each other, making allowances for each other's faults because of your love. Always keep yourselves united in the Holy Spirit, and bind yourselves together with peace" (Ephesians 4:1-3). That to-do list is both instructive and motivating. Pause for moment and ask, *Am I pure in my relationships with other Christians? Do I even try? Is it a goal of mine to be humble, gentle, patient, united and peaceful with fellow believers in Jesus Christ?*

The next chapter, Ephesians 5, follows with a stop-doing list: "Let there be no sexual immorality, impurity, or greed among you. Such sins have no place among God's people. Obscene stories, foolish talk, and coarse jokes—these are not for you. . . . You can be sure that no immoral, impure or greedy person will inherit the Kingdom of Christ and of God" (verses 3-5). Wow!

With God's help, I promise to practice purity in thought and action. That's my to-do list for today—and every day.

Signature Stop-doing List

What shall I put on today's "stop-doing" list? Some readers are scratching their heads, trying to identify a life problem that needs correction. Congratulations. Does the word *pride* give a hint?

For those hundreds of thousands of us a little less deluded, the question is more like weeding my garden. It's not "Are there any weeds?" but "At which end of the garden shall I start, and will I ever overcome all these unbecoming, unwelcome intruders?"

Here's a suggestion that will condense your stop-doing list down to one item. A stop-doing list of 13 sins or faults could be too much to remember, let alone pull off. But a list of one is manageable. I'm suggesting that you identify the biggest weed, the weed with the deepest roots, the weed that infiltrates the rest of the garden.

The King James Version of the Bible calls this the *besetting sin.* "Let us lay aside every weight, and the sin which doth so easily beset us" (Hebrews 12:1, KJV). That may sound a little archaic. Instead, we'll call it a *signature sin.*

> *The King James Version of the Bible calls this the* beset-*ting sin. That may sound a little archaic. Instead, we'll call it a* signature sin.

If you can't identify your signature sin and wonder if you have one, Jesus gave this question to help you: "Why worry about the speck in your friend's eye when you have a log in your own?" (Matthew 7:3). Each spring my garden fills up with volunteer Maple and Box Elder tree shoots, which I must pull or hoe. At the end of the garden is a tall Box Elder tree that a neighbor tells me was a volunteer that no one uprooted 20 years ago. Now it has an 18-inch trunk. Neighbor John chides me when I'm weeding my garden: "While you're at it, pull up that Box Elder." He wonders why I fuss over and pull the little weeds while ignoring the besetting log—precisely the question in Jesus' mind.

Your signature sin is a fault that sprang up, probably years ago, and is growing from weedy sprout to sapling to the sinful tree trunk in your life. You've learned to accept it and work around it, but Jesus still wants it pulled out. We are to quit nitpicking the minor tares in the lives of others and uproot or cut down the signature sin in our own lives.

How to Spell PURITY

David conquered the Philistine armies by slaying Goliath, who stood out like a log among toothpicks (1 Samuel 17). Goliath, the pride and hero of the Philistine army, was nine feet tall and wore a coat of mail that weighed 125 pounds. Goliath was the signature soldier of the Philistine army. Had David's strategy been to find and fight the weakest enemy in a uniform and work his way up to Goliath, the results would have been far different from the dramatic sling victory. David wouldn't have lasted long, and Goliath and the Philistines would never have been chased from the land.

David went after the "biggest and baddest" of the bully Philistines—the signature soldier, the besetting brawler. He won because he had the right battle plan and was fighting with God's help.

That's what I'm asking you to do. And here is a step-by-step plan (a list, we might call it!) to get you started overcoming your signature sin. Let's spell purity this way:

P—*Put your name by your signature sin.*

At 12-step meetings, such as Alcoholics Anonymous, the first step is calling out your name with your signature addiction: "Hi, I'm John, and I'm an alcoholic." That is a breakthrough moment. The apostle Paul often began his testimony: "Hi, I'm Paul, and I was a persecutor of the church." That was his signature sin. Tax collector Levi probably began to follow Christ by owning up to his signature sin of cheating citizens out of their money.

Try it on for size:

"I'm Fred, and I'm addicted to pornography."

"I'm Francis, and I steal from my company."

"I'm Chris, and I cut people down behind their backs whenever I get a chance."

U—*Unmask who you are before God.*
Isaiah was a religious man who wanted to be an authentic, pure believer. At a crisis time in his nation's history, Isaiah was praying and had a vision of heaven being opened. He saw angels who shouted, "Holy, holy, holy is the Lord."

Isaiah's response was not, "Oh boy, this is great!" Rather he cried out, "Woe is me! For I am undone" (or exposed and doomed) "because I am a man of unclean lips" (Isaiah 6:5, KJV).

In the presence of God and the angels, Isaiah was unmasked, and he confessed his signature sin. God has promised that "if we confess our sins, he is faithful and just to forgive us our sins, and to cleanse us from all unrighteousness" (1 John 1:9, KJV). God did just that for Isaiah. "Then flew one of the seraphim unto me, having a live coal in his hand, which he had taken with the tongs from off the altar. And he laid it upon my mouth, and said, Lo, this hath touched thy lips, and thine iniquity is taken away, and thy sin purged" (Isaiah 6:6–7, KJV). Isaiah became a great spokesman, a prophet and writer, for God. But first he needed to unmask his signature sin.

R—*Replace old patterns with new possibilities.*
There is an East Coast pro basketball player with great talent and a propensity to get into trouble. The league consensus is that he needs to run with a new crowd. Whenever he's with his old buddies, he falls

into familiar patterns, and the police usually have to get involved.

Signature sins are never loners; they have friends and a recognizable modus operandi. Accomplices may include actual people or habits or use of time and money. If your signature sin is addiction to television soaps, you need to reprogram that time of day. Volunteer those hours to a service or ministry. Get a part-time job. Work out at the gym. Study your Bible. But stay away from the TV. Get away from the old crowd.

I—*Identify Scriptures that keep you focused.*
The psalmist David was a master at this: "I have hidden your word in my heart, that I might not sin against you," he wrote (Psalm 119:11). Memorize Scripture that reminds you of how special you are to God or how Jesus died to set you free from your sins. Meditate on God's Word. Carry with you verses of power and love and hope. Contact your church or pastor—or call 1-800-224-2735 to order *The Little Scripture Pack for Practicing Purity*. The Word of God is sure to help you.

T—*Trust a friend to help you.*
Be a friend to another. We are all sinners, dysfunctional at times, and in need of accountability. Paul the apostle was Philemon's friend, a relationship that allowed each to monitor and mentor the other. When Paul suspected Philemon might not treat another in a Christian manner, he wrote, "If you consider me your partner, give him the same welcome you would give me if I were coming" (Philemon 17). Paul was in prison at the time, so he handled this by mail. He suggested, "Please keep a guest room ready for me, for I am hoping that God will answer your prayers and let me return to you soon" (Philemon 22).

Who is the person you can trust to encourage you with your stop-doing list, the person you would take into your home at a moment's notice if the need arose? If you don't have one, you're missing out on a key to wiping out that signature sin.

Y—*Yell for joy when you get it right.*

The next time you watch a football game, pay attention to the opening kickoff. Whichever team feels they outdid the other on the first play will celebrate, high-five, chest- or head-butt, and strut. They haven't won the game. But they've got one play right, and they deserve to yell about it. When you find yourself, with God's grace, ruling over a former signature sin, give God the glory and yell for joy!

That is how you spell PURITY, Gini. May God strengthen you, and all the Ginis and Genes across the land, to reject compromise and live as a person of wonderful promise.

Whatever your name is, you are special to God, and you can reign in life over even that besetting signature sin. Let the signature sin be replaced with personal purity. May you be known by purity in thought and action and bring glory to your Father in heaven.

That's a promise worth keeping by a person of promise.

"The Circle"
by Janet Burroughs Woodward

A little party, a meeting chance,
A boy, a girl, a second glance.
A lovely evening, a long walk home,
A pleasant talk, some time alone.

A double date with friends we share;
A movie show, and then we pair.
A hiding spot, we meet like this,
A turned off place, a turned on kiss.

A quiet thrill, a little sin,
A first impulse to do again.
A few more dates, a better place,
An argument makes bitter taste.

A make-up kiss, throw in a squeeze;
A blushing girl, a playful tease.
A mom, a dad disrupt the fun;
A guy, a girl, a secret run.

A better place, a better time;
An ideal spot for immoral crime.
A broken shack, a warming fire,
A growing taste for lust desire.

A wooden bed, a dirt floor dried;
A hunger to be satisfied.
Words of love you will not heed
Till satisfaction's guaranteed.

Later on a long walk back,
A secret hiding in the shack.
Secret meeting, a lover's fight,
Of what was wrong and what is right.

A broken heart, no make-up kiss;
A preview look at what you'll miss.
The thrill is gone and no more life
In the dream of being man and wife.

But something's there to remind you of
Your hiding place and selfish love.
New life begins, a shameful start.
To tear and slowly break your heart.

When it's over you'll start again
But this time be aware of sin.
Try to make a better life;
Meet a guy and be his wife.

A little party, a meeting chance;
A boy, a girl, a second glance.

"The Holy Spirit is not given to those who have it all together spiritually; He is given to enable us to get it together spiritually! I'm struck with Paul's words: 'but I say, walk by the spirit and you will not carry out the desire of the flesh' (Gal. 5:16). Notice the sequence. Paul does not say that if we stop carrying out the desires of the flesh we will walk in the spirit; rather, if we walk in the Spirit, we will not fulfill the desires of the flesh! That order makes an incredible difference."
—*Erwin Lutzer*, How to Say No to a Stubborn Habit

"Resolved, never to do anything which I would be afraid to do if it were the last hour of my life."
—*Jonathan Edwards*

"I pray thee, Lord, to cleanse me now from sin,
Fulfill Thy promise, make me pure within,
Fill me with fire where once I burned with shame,
Grant my desire to magnify thy name."
—*J. Edwin Orr*

"He that covereth his sins shall not prosper, but whoso confesseth and forsaketh them shall have mercy."
—*Proverbs 28:13*, KJV

CHAPTER 4

The Family Story

*With God's help, I promise to make
family relationships a priority.*

There were rumors that Judy had a brother. Rumors
also persist of sightings of Sasquatch alive and well
in the Oregon mountains. Late night TV's camper
video clips made Bigfoot more credible than Judy's
brother. There were no Texas sightings of Judy's
brother at birthday parties or graduations. There
were no video clips of this brother with the family
vacations or at Thanksgiving gatherings. At church,
Judy spoke of her brother in affectionate and glow-
ing terms. Her story was that she had a wonderful
brother who loved her, who was kind and good.

Children often create a make-believe brother or
friend to play with. They sing to their imaginary
friend and take walks with him or her. Parents smile
indulgently when food is shared. Everyone knows
that such friends are forgotten long before adoles-
cence. Real flesh-and-bone friends began to show
concern for Judy over her imaginary brother. Should
they recommend professional help? Could they trick
her into visiting a counselor? What they didn't know
was that her brother had a good excuse: I was busy.

I was too busy with family to have time for family.
My wife and I were raising our own children. With
school and church and work and athletics, we didn't

have time for aunts and uncles. Dad died, and my widowed mother needed plenty of care. Who had what it took to make a trip to Texas? Not one trip in nine years. I can give you a trainload of explanations, but when the explaining is done, I must still face the plain truth that this part of family was not my priority. And for many, this neglect caused pain: the vacuity of having a brother and uncle who didn't value them enough to show up for significant occasions.

My brother Bob died unexpectedly at the age of forty-one. In the previous twenty years, Bob and I saw each other four or five times. There were always excuses—even reasons—why we didn't get together. He was in the military, and I was a missionary or pastor. We were family, but we compromised our priorities. At his funeral, I wished I had buried my excuses and spent more time with my brother. I felt the sorrow of regret that there would be no more tomorrows, no more "some other times" to enjoy Bob. It's foolish to reckon that a job has to be done now, but family will always be there, waiting for you.

> *At his funeral, I wished I had buried my excuses and spent more time with my brother.*

Bob's widow remarried, and Chuck and Hanne are both family and friends. We live in Illinois, and they live a thousand miles away in Georgia. It remains a determined effort to make family a priority. Some of us work harder at it than others. Jesus did.

Jesus had parents and relatives he made a priority. He was part of a great earthly family with aunts, uncles, and cousins. This family went to synagogue together and even traveled from Nazareth to Jerusalem for great religious festivals (Luke 2:41–50). Every year they went to the Feast of the Passover with "their kinfolk and acquaintances" (verse 44, KJV). This was a combined spiritual pilgrimage and family reunion. What a splendid concept!

Taking those festivals as a cue, our family—extended to aunts, uncles, cousins, and schnauzers—will spend a week this summer at a Christian conference center in North Carolina. We'll combine spiritual growth with family fun and storytelling.

A first-time family project to be completed by this reunion is a family calendar. Judy is collecting current family pictures from the extended family with birthdays and anniversary dates. I'll scan the pictures and type the dates into a computer. Of course, when I print and present the calendar, I'll lose all my excuses for forgetting special occasions. No project is perfect.

Recounting Family History

I wish I could spin our family story for you, because storytelling links us to the greater whole of family life. I'd love to tell you how we confirmed that Nancy is a descendant of Daniel Boone; or how my great grandfather Leander Clark came back from the '49 California Gold Rush to settle in Iowa and later came to a personal commitment to Christ at the age of fifty-seven; or how my niece Renate won a trip to Hawaii this year; or how the house filled with smoke when we forgot we were boiling baby bottles—today. But these are our stories, our family connections, our history that ties us together, even if we live hundreds of miles apart.

You have your stories. Let them live. Alex Haley, the author of *Roots*, reminds us, "The family is our refuge and springboard; nourished on it, we can advance to new horizons. In every conceivable manner, the family is link to the past, bridge to the future."

Telling the family story nurtures belonging and continuity. It builds a frame for my family picture and a context for my life's character. I am the product of my family history. I'm not bound by that, but I'm influenced by it. My sister Judy and brother-in-law Larry were discussing with Nancy and me how our parents' marriages affected our marriages. In the middle of a marital verbal wrestlemania, Larry will look at Judy and say, "I'm not your father," and she'll retort, "And I'm not your mother." It would take a three-volume family biography to explain that fully. The summary is that two divergent family stories merged in their marriage, each bringing style, expectations, and some baggage. Knowing the family story puts that in perspective, helps us understand our behavior, steers us toward making allowances, and shows us where we need to grow or grow up.

> *If you struggle as a conversationalist, your ace-in-the-hole is to inquire about family history.*

If you struggle as a conversationalist, your ace-in-the-hole is to inquire about family history. Last week I hired a man to trim two trees in my yard. I'm not afraid of heights, but I avoid situations where I can fall a long way with sharp tools in my hands. Andy was the best tree trimmer I ever saw work. As I wrote the check, I asked where he was from. A half-hour later I knew that he was the oldest of nine children, what his parents were like, how he continued to relate to them and his siblings, and when Christ graced their family. Yesterday he was working in the neighborhood again and came back to the house to see if I was satisfied with his work. I asked another question and learned how he became a tree trimmer and that he was taking care of his mom while his dad went to Wisconsin for a medical appointment. Andy needed to tell his story. It was more than conversation. It was life affirmation. Life made sense to him as he told his family story. Relating the story made family the priority in his life.

Delores Curran asks:

> Why is it that the young in some families grow up, leave home for college or work a thousand miles away, and, for all practical purposes, sever any emotional ties with their family of origin, while the young of another family, similar in most respects to the first, retain strong emotional ties to their family? In the first, a family is regarded as a place to leave, a discarded nest to be returned to only at obligatory times like holidays, illnesses, and death, while in the second the family is considered to be a lifelong base of love and support.[1]

Nancy and I come from traditions too much like the former. If it's not too late—and I know it isn't—we want to change our family perspective to the latter "lifelong base of love and support." *With God's help, I promise to make family relationships a priority.* This promise is an appointment with loved ones.

The Tension: Independence and Belonging
There is tension at every great doctrine or truth. The tension here is that Scripture instructs us to leave our parents and to cleave to our spouse while teaching us to honor our parents and widowed mothers

throughout life. I see this tension lived out as my young adult children yearn to be independent of Nancy and me yet retain a strong need to belong to us. The problem is that some families have so few ties, and others are smothering and suffocating.

Jesus embraced the tension of independence and belonging. As early as his twelfth year, he took steps toward autonomy when he stayed in the temple long after the rest of the family had begun the trip back home (Luke 2:43–50). Yet at thirty he was still bonded to family and remained so until he died.

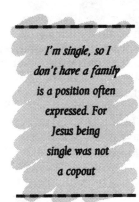

I'm single, so I don't have a family is a position often expressed. For Jesus being single was not a copout

Jesus clearly saw family as a link to the past and a bridge to the future, not a temporary arrangement to flee. It is common at weddings to hear words like these: "Marriage is an honorable estate, instituted in the time of innocence, signifying to us the mystical union between Christ and his church. Which holy estate Christ adorned and beautified with his presence at the first miracle which he wrought in Cana of Galilee." That initial miracle was the changing of water to wine at a wedding reception when the original supply had embarrassingly been exhausted.

Jesus was single, but he valued mother, home, family, and marriage. *I'm single, so I don't have a family* is a position often expressed and probably believed. For Jesus, being single was not a copout.

Jesus lived at home until he was thirty. Lest you think I'm suggesting he was overdue to move out, let me remind you that Joseph is never mentioned during Jesus' adult years. We conclude from this that Mary was a widow before fifty years of age. Jesus, as the eldest son, would assume much responsibility for the care of his mother. Indeed, from the cross he continued to make arrangements for her provision and security. Jesus said to the apostle John, "Here is your mother," referring to Mary (John 19:27, NIV).

At thirty, Jesus was ready to launch his public ministry. He saw no conflict between public and private duties, and he chose a humble home to begin his work of renown. We have no record that either the bride or groom was an immediate relative, but they could have been. Jesus' mother was so involved in the catering of the wedding that when the wine supply ran out, she felt personally responsible.

Mary must either have been family or close enough to the wedding party to be "just like family," like my Aunt Erma in Ohio. I was surprised to learn one day in the second grade that Aunt Erma was not really an aunt at all; she was my mother's closest friend. I never thought any less of her. As an honorary aunt, she received a special place in our home. Jesus' family included natural relatives plus the expanded family of faith and friends.

Jesus, as a single man about to begin a new career, attended and supported this family wedding, never looking for any excuse to do otherwise. From time to time during his ministry, Jesus' eternal glory burst forth in remarkable manifestations. He planned the first such occasion not in front of a vast crowd, but within a family gathering. He made family relationships a priority.

To Jesus, the family was the alphabet of revelation: fatherhood, bride and groom, adoption, new birth, travail, love, sacrifice, reverence, obedience. When God established the family in the Garden of Eden, he had not only the health of society in view but the revelation of himself in Jesus Christ. "To all who believed on him and accepted him, he gave the right to become the children of God" (John 1:12).

The Legend of the Lawn

When Christine was three, she wanted a sandbox in the backyard. "There goes the lawn," Dad said. "We'll have the neighbor's kids here all the time, stomping and running and throwing sand. It'll kill the grass for sure."

Christine's mother said, "It'll come back."

At five, Christine wanted a swing set, complete with a high slide and bars to climb on. As Dad bolted it together, he moaned, "Our backyard will look like a school playground. When it rains it'll look more like a pigpen than a lawn. This'll kill the grass for sure."

And Mother said, "It'll come back."

Three years later, Dad was setting up a swimming pool and complaining. "I see kids splashing water and chasing and sliding across the lawn. Our yard will look like home plate after a rainstorm. It'll kill the grass."

Christine's mother smiled. "It'll come back."

At twelve, Christine invited the Girl Scout troop over for a campout. As the tents went up and the tug-of-war rope was stretched, Dad sighed, "Why do I bother with fertilizers and aerators? I might as well put the mower in storage. They'll kill the grass." Mom winked. "It'll come back."

Christine and several high-school sophomore soccer teammates used the backyard as a practice field. Brown divots appeared like the pox . . . except for the goal area, which was a giant fifteen-foot divot. Dad shook his head in resignation. "I don't ask for much, only a lawn the neighbors won't mock."

Mother consoled him. "It'll come back, dear."

He finally had the lawn he wanted: grass like the greens at Augusta, Georgia, edged in weedless flower beds. Dad stood in the backyard nervous, uneasy, not enjoying a bit of it. With a lump in his throat, he asked Mother, "She will come back, won't she?"

Told and retold, the legend of the lawn helps us recognize the compromise in valuing possessions over family. It's easy to think the family is a priority, to claim it's the priority, but sometimes hard to release "mistress" priorities. Your priority is what you live for, and love and adore. When a dad explodes in wrath because a kindergarten daughter nicked the car finish, what holds prior claim in his affection? Many a parent who has never had a sexual affair still has a mistress with job or sports or lawn. In the legend, Christine was the priority with Dad. He whined a bit over the grass, but at every stage of life Christine's needs came first and the grass was sacrificed. And in the end he knew that family had always been everything, and grass was just grass.

Is there a mistress in your life claiming priority in time or money over spouse and children? Will you resolve to be like Christine's mom or dad? *With God's help, I vow to make family relationships a priority over lawns and cars or any other temptation.* This is a family appointment for tomorrow by a person of promise.

Authenticating

Generous displays of luxurious jewelry were the trademarks of my Great-aunt Belle's ensembles. Uncle Albert had been an independent grocer in Jackson, Michigan, and our image of him was of grand financial success. After sixty years of marriage, Uncle Al and Aunt Belle died within a few months of each other. The diamonds in Aunt Belle's rings, when appraised for estate settlement, were found to be "paste." I doubt Aunt Belle ever suspected that her husband was giving her compromised diamonds. I'm also sure she never received certificates of authenticity from any jewelry store with these heirloom gifts. There was more than a little disappointment within the family when we learned that all that sparkles is not diamond.

Have you ever been certified authentic? Strangers you impress might judge you so. But how would your family rate you?

Jesus' authenticity was both within himself and through his family. Jesus was being independently authentic when he declared, "I am the way, the truth, and the life." But he put that authenticity in family context with the next breath: "No one can come to the Father except through me" (John 14:6). "There are many rooms in my Father's home, and I am going to prepare a place for you," he had just promised (verse 2). This unmarried man lived and breathed home and family.

Jesus was simultaneously the one who preexisted eternally "in the beginning with God" (John 1:2) and was born "a mighty savior from the royal line of his servant David." (Luke 1:69). He was true to himself, yet his authenticity was also in his family story. You must be authentic before God, whether or not others believe in you. Yet your intrinsic value will be affirmed in all decades through your family.

Adopting Others as Family

If you don't have a family, you'll have to create one.
There are many who claim no family ties. Their relatives died in war or are still living in the old country. The reasons for loneliness—even isolation—are
many, but they needn't continue. An excellent place
to find or create an adopted
family is church. I have
decades-long family-type
relationships with several
who are related to me not
by blood or marriage but by
faith in Jesus Christ. Such
relationships need the same
kind of attention, time, and
deliberate cultivation that
I'm suggesting for all family
ties.

> *I have decades-long
> family-type relation-
> ships with several
> who are related to
> me not by blood or
> marriage but by
> faith in Jesus Christ.*

I'm especially conscious of finding authentic value
in family, because our two children are adopted.
Now twenty-five and twenty-three, Amy and Larry
have struggled through memorable history, searching
for their authentic places in life. Amy sought authenticity through love, while Larry sought it through
success. Children of adoption, of divorce, and of
single parents will intuitively appreciate this. *Who am
I* and *Where do I belong?* are less obvious to those
raised outside a traditional nuclear family.
Ultimately this answer must be found in our relationship with God through Jesus Christ: "I am a
child of God, and I belong to his family."

Yet earthly family cannot be discounted. Our family
traditions are more important because of adoption,
not less. They stabilize authenticity. We hung and
filled Christmas stockings for the kids all the way

through high school, because authentic belonging was still a pursuit more than a settled given. When the family is other than the romantic model (and it almost always is), we need to double our efforts to bring authenticity through family connections and traditions.

Sandy, a fifty-something single lady whose parents have passed away, moved to Wheaton, Illinois, last month to reestablish ties to cousins and extended relatives. She wants to know them as more than names on Christmas cards. She is ready to trade in 30 years of wandering independence for an authentic seat at a family Christmas dinner.

Traditions and rituals give the family a sense of reality and strength in a mobile and unrooted society. Here is a partial list of traditions from just one family.

• Youngest child always blows out the candles
• Dad gives kids "dutch rubs" on the crowns of their heads when he says goodnight
• When a child is twelve, he or she becomes responsible for washing the car
• Wednesday is leftover night
• Waffles every Sunday morning
• Mom hides the family valentines
• Easter eggs are dyed on Good Friday night
• A taking-down-the-tree party on January 1
• Once a year family ice-skating—no friends allowed
• Celebrate the cat's birthday
• Clean out the basement together the first day of summer vacation, ending with hot dogs cooked outside
• Leaving notes on the refrigerator
• Pretending to avoid Mom's goodnight kiss
• Dad and boys go fishing on Memorial Day weekend, Mom and girls go shopping

- Each child gets to talk to Grandma long distance without anyone listening
- Mother's and Father's Day cards made from scratch
- Visit Aunt Ellen in the nursing home after church on holidays[2]

I encourage you to make a list of your own family traditions and rituals. You have more than you realize, and each fosters feelings of authenticity and belonging. Would you believe that our family goes bowling once a year—on Christmas night? I think my son would fly from any place in the world to open presents Christmas morning and go bowling Christmas night. *With God's help, I promise to make family relationships a priority by participating in our rituals.* This promise is a family appointment for weeks and years to come.

Daily Priority
Today is the only day you will ever have. If family is to be priority, it won't happen yesterday or tomorrow but today. Think of what you can do today to make a family member feel special. This doesn't need to involve an expensive gift, and it won't have to take five hours. But get into the habit of blessing your family every day, and think of your family with an extended view.

We are progressing from "I'll make my family a priority" to "I'll make one family member a priority *today.*" We are moving from the general to the specific, from the concept to the assignment. Now, what will you do today? Since you know your family better and have had your highly creative moments, you'll think my suggestions meager and elementary. These are just to prime the pump.

We can learn from the above list of family traditions. Some rituals, such as bedtime routines, were daily. Others, like Sunday pancakes, were weekly. Many were annual. We want to major on the daily with a few weekly traditions tossed in.

- E-mail a cousin a "praying for you" note.
- Mail a family picture and story to an uncle.
- Wash the dishes (if that's not your chore).
- Take a child to a park, ice-cream shop, or anyplace special.
- Early in the morning, hold the hand of a spouse, child, or parent and pray for God's blessing on that day.
- Come home with a "Here's what God did in my life" story instead of a work complaint.
- Call a relative to say hi and ask how he or she is doing.
- Learn a new "knock-knock" joke for younger children.
- Buy an elderly parent a music cassette or CD.
- Praise a child and vow not to criticize for a day.
- Fix a broken toy.
- Schedule a quick trip to visit a relative or close friend.

Write these daily family touches in a log, and deem each touch a delight, a treasured moment, or just plain fun. Mainstay Church Resources (1-800-224-2735) can supply you with a 50-day journal to help you record your daily acts of kindness to your family. Or you may use your Day Timer, diary, or notebook.

Larry and Judy moved from Texas to Michigan four years ago, so instead of 1,200 miles, we are only 350 miles apart. Last Friday they drove here to meet our latest grandchild, Zachary, and returned home Saturday. If we are to make family a priority, we must extend the hand, say the words, write the notes, buy the gifts, and drive the miles.

With God's help, I promise to make family relationships a priority TODAY. This is an appointment to be kept by a person of promise, before tomorrow.

Family Vows

Families are created through vows—wedding vows in particular—and births. Did you know that vows, or covenants, come in two classifications?

First, there are conditional vows. I told Nancy last week, "If it doesn't rain Saturday, I'll transplant those bushes." It rained, but I didn't have to dig in the rain, because my commitment was conditional.

> *Did you know that vows come in two classifications? First, there are conditional vows. The family model is unconditional.*

The other kind of covenant is unconditional. "For better or worse; for richer or poorer, in sickness and in health, till death do us part" establishes a commitment without conditions, without mitigating circumstances, without escape clauses. The highest and holiest covenants are always unconditional. In the Old Testament, God told Moses that if the people would keep his laws, he would bless and protect them. The Old Testament was a blessing conditioned on behavior. The New Testament promises salvation not conditioned on law keeping but unconditional through faith in Christ's death for our sins and resurrection unto eternal life.

The family model is unconditional. I met with a couple last month who were struggling with a rebellious adopted teenager. They were seeking help in sorting through their options. I first reminded them that adoption was as unconditional as natural birth.

Their options were not "out of" but "through" this difficult time.

I told them about the question Jesus asked: "If a shepherd has one hundred sheep, and one wanders away and is lost, what will he do? Won't he leave the ninety-nine others and go out into the hills to search for the lost one? And if he finds it, he will surely rejoice over it more than over the ninety-nine that didn't wander away!" (Matthew 18:12–13). Jesus said that was how our heavenly Father feels toward perishing people. In a business context, you would never leave ninety-nine sheep to go find one that was lost. But in a healthy family context, a father would always leave ninety-nine relatives or friends to go after one lost son or daughter. He's bound to that child unconditionally by love and family vows.

Respect your marriage vows. Respect the vows of others. Unconditionally love your family, and every day show that love to one or more. When siblings and cousins tell the family story, you won't be a rumor, an invisible Sasquatch. The time you stumbled and fell with the birthday cake will be told and retold, but it'll be told with love and humor.

With God's help, I promise to make family relationships a priority. This promise is an appointment for today and tomorrow and the next day, one to be savored with fidelity as long as God gives you someone to call family.

It's a promise worth keeping by people of promise.

"A Child Learns"

If a child lives with hostility,
He learns to fight.
If a child lives with criticism,
He learns to condemn.
If a child lives with fear,
He learns to be apprehensive.
If a child lives with jealousy,
He learns to hate.
If a child lives with self-pity,
He learns to be sorry for himself.
If a child lives with encouragement,
He learns self-confidence and integrity.
If a child lives with praise,
He learns to be appreciative.
If a child lives with acceptance,
He learns to love.
If a child lives with approval,
He learns to like himself.
If a child lives with fairness,
He learns justice.
If a child lives with honesty,
He learns what truth is.
If a child lives with friendliness,
He learns that the world is a nice place in which
  to live.
—*Author unknown*

"Home is the field where love must bear its best
fruit."
—*J. Wilbur Chapman*

"Valuing is exactly what the patriarchs in the Old
Testament did in blessing their children with the
family blessing. They were attaching high value to

them. We do the same when we bless our children, spouse, or friends, and every person today needs the blessing to feel truly loved and secure about himself or herself. This concept of valuing another person is so important that we believe it can be found at the heart of every healthy relationship."
—*Gary Smalley & John Trent*, The Gift of the Blessing

"Family first shouldn't be interpreted to mean 'family only.' Human beings aren't meant to live isolated lives. We need to interact with others. One of the main themes Kim and I stress to our children is maintaining great passion for your personal pursuits and great compassion for others. We are all part of a larger family called humankind."
—*Mike Singletary*, Daddy's Home at Last

CHAPTER 5

The Nostalgic Method

*With God's help, I promise to support
the ministry of my church and pastor.*

People often want to know where I'm originally
from. What spurs this curiosity I'm reluctant to pos-
tulate, but all I can tell them is "Jackson, Michigan."
With misty eyes and a salivating smile, they pre-
dictably respond, "Oh yes, the home of The Parlor."

I suppose everyone in Michigan has been to The
Parlor; they come in busloads from Detroit and
Lansing. If you're from Oklahoma or New York and
have lived a sheltered life, there is a slight possibility
you have never heard of The Parlor. The Parlor is the
best ice cream place in the world. It's been that way
since the '50s.

Anyone who has been to the parlor is nostalgic for
it. Nostalgia is the true test of greatness—or a poor
memory. I choose to believe the first option. You
know how great something is when you grow nostalgic for it.

When I think of my hometown, I'm nostalgic for
The Parlor, Cascades Park, and my church. The
Cascades is to parks what The Parlor is to ice cream
shops. The Cascades is the park of parks, with hills,
streams and lagoons, fish and birds, and the roman-
tically beautiful Cascade Falls. A park is just a park
until you grow nostalgic for it. The Boston

Commons, for example, evokes great emotion in easterners. Of course, that's only because they haven't been to Cascades Park.

When I visit Jackson in the summer, I get orange-pineapple ice cream from The Parlor, savor a long walk at the Cascades, and go to church. My best elementary-school-age memories are of my church. Ditto for my junior and senior high years. Church was the best part of my life. School was okay, but I've never been nostalgic for any of my academic institutions. My friend Jim loves to tell school stories and grows misty-eyed, like a boy for his puppy. I had a dog, and I cried when Taffy died, but I'm not nostalgic for her. It's my church experiences I'd relive if I could. I loved the music, the pastors and teachers, the evangelism and sense of God's presence, the love and encouragement. One of the best measures of a church's greatness is whether anyone is nostalgic for it, or will be nostalgic for it in ten years from now.

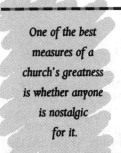

One of the best measures of a church's greatness is whether anyone is nostalgic for it.

Shari, a friend and coworker, is nostalgic for Ward Presbyterian Church in Detroit, Michigan. When she moved to Illinois, she spent a year trying to find a clone of her home church. Ward Presbyterian is a large church, near megachurch stature, but it isn't the size she misses. Ward was the church where she was discipled and became a strong Christian. She loves her pastor and often speaks of her singles group ministry. Every memory is spiritually rich, full of blessing from God's hand to her impressionable heart.

Dotty's home church in western Nebraska has always been a small, farm family congregation of two or three dozen dear souls. Dotty sings the praises of this church at every opportunity and visits a couple of times a year, even though it's a thousand miles away. She never comes back disappointed. They still love her there and roll out the red carpet for her infrequent returns.

The next promise is: *With God's help, I promise to support the ministry of my church and pastor.* How do you do that? Here's the key: Help build a church that the congregation someday will hold nostalgically in memory. It's as simple as that. The functions of your church must be the expression of biblical criteria for worship, discipleship, fellowship, and evangelism. Within the framework of Christ's agenda, learn to support your church in a manner that will evoke warm church memories when you look back. If your church is wonderfully blessed today, continue those key elements that warm hearts and bring God's anointing.

The nostalgic method of supporting a church has a lot going for it. For one thing, you can't argue with it. When a friend says, "I always loved the music in the church where I grew up," you can't say, "No, you didn't." A better response would be to say to yourself, *Our church today must have music people can connect with emotionally.*

The Nostalgic Method also screens out bad memories and whiny complaints that no one wants to hear anyway. Warm church memories are just that—treasured recollections of spiritually rich times. If you only want to avoid mishaps, major on what went wrong in the past. But if you want to do a thing right and experience success and blessing, screen out the unpleasant and focus on all that is "true and honorable and right. Think about things that are pure and lovely and admirable. Think about things that are excellent and worthy of praise. Keep putting into practice all you learned" (Philippians 4:8–9). Nostalgia is a path to success, because it guides us accurately to what is healthy and works. Someday the Nostalgic Method may be as famous as the Socratic Method!

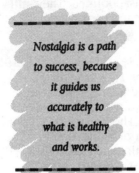

Nostalgia is a path to success, because it guides us accurately to what is healthy and works.

Our Lord was deeply concerned over the authenticity of his churches. In the Revelation of Jesus Christ, he sent letters to seven churches, some of which had been compromised to the verge of being not only imperfect, but inauthentic. Jesus issued a warning to shape up, or "I will come and remove your lampstand from its place among the churches" (Revelation 2:5).

Did you know that Jesus began his appraisal using the Nostalgic Method? Listen to his letter to the church in Ephesus: "I have seen your hard work and your patient endurance. I know you don't tolerate evil people." These are affirming words. "But," he continues, "I have this complaint against you. You don't love me or each other as you did at the first. Look how far you have fallen from your first love! Turn back to me again and work as you did at first" (Revelation 2:2–5). The Ephesian church had decades of history when Jesus wrote to them through the apostle John. Jesus had warm memories for the early days of passionate love within that church. He wanted the younger generation to love him and the gospel as fervently as their grandparents did. That is employing the Nostalgic Method as a guide for church support.

We need to participate in church life in a way that will bring power and blessing today and warm church memories tomorrow. Last Sunday we sang the chorus, "In my church, Lord, be glorified, be glorified today." To God there should "be glory in the church and in Christ Jesus throughout all generations" (Ephesians 3:21, NIV). God is gloried from one generation to the next when each generation looks back on its church days with gratitude and praise.

The *You Need to Know* Christian television program taped sixty-second "Warm Church Memories" by international Christian leaders. College presidents, authors, and evangelists all recalled warm impressions from Sunday school teachers, youth clubs, and Christian camps. From the show, I've excerpted the Warm Church Memories of some of Christendom's currently esteemed voices. We'll employ the Nostalgic Method to our own church involvement as we enjoy and evaluate the memories these honored church leaders have carried, often from childhood to maturity. This is critical: For the church to continue to prosper, our youth and adults must carry an excitement for all their current church experiences into the future. Older teens who hold sour memories of boring services and grouchy leaders will be the first to drop out. But the youth who savor nostalgic memories of loving leaders and services full of the presence of Jesus will hold to the faith, lead the church, and pass their trust in Christ on to their children.

Nostalgic Church Family Memories
The people of a church must work at being a caring church family. "You are members of God's family. We are his house," the apostle Paul wrote (Ephesians 2:19). Your church must have the atmosphere of a kind and healthy family that supports and celebrates life. In smaller churches, this familial feeling

may permeate the entire congregation. In larger churches, the family atmosphere is often experienced in a class, ministry team, or small group.

Someone suggested, "You might be a committee member if a church picnic is no picnic." Picnics and potlucks, banquets and barbecues certainly take preparation. Are they worth the effort? Pastor, media preacher, and author Tony Evans fondly remembers his church picnics as living models of a congregation enjoying itself as a family. The picnics were building blocks in the faith walk of one now respected as a contemporary prophet to the church.

> I remember our annual church picnic. During that time we got together as an extended family. That's the thing that comes out of it, family. Everybody loved and cared for one another, sort of like a family reunion. I never forgot those warm times of being together, praising God and having fun. That showed me that Christianity wasn't a drab, irrelevant activity, but it could emanate into exciting times together as the extended family of God. That's one of my fond memories of church growing up.

In addition to the weekly Hebrew Sabbaths, God provided a series of celebrations throughout the Jewish year that provided extended family fellowship along with focus on a spiritual truth. The Feast of Tabernacles was like a week-long family camp. If your church schedules a family camp, your good-natured participation will contribute to others' nostalgic memories. In my last church, we held huge barbecues on the church grounds the Sunday afternoons of several holiday weekends. These became healthy and anticipated church traditions. As I write, I can recall the smell of barbecue smoke, see children chasing each other and laughing, and hear stories being shared. Attendance at Lord's Day services is core to the Christian walk. But we also need family fellowship experiences. Church picnics and camps are blessings, even when the mosquitoes swarm and it rains.

Families are a lot more fun when there is love and humor to cover a little indiscretion. Television producer and host Rod Hembry began his life-changing church memory with a wordless smile that took three seconds. Then he said:

> *As I write, I can recall the smell of barbecue smoke, see children chasing each other and laughing, and hear stories being shared.*

> At fourteen I was sitting at the back of the church and my father was preaching. I decided to bend paper clips so I could fire them across the church sanctuary. I had a great rubber band in my pocket. This thing was powerful. I pulled back the paper clip in the rubber band and fired away, and it hit a board member right in the back of the head. I realized at that moment I could get into some serious trouble. You know what he did? He turned around and smiled at me, and then he kept listening to the sermon. That board member kept me out of trouble. That is my Warm Church Memory.

That was a teeter-totter instant when law could wound or grace could build a lad. With that smile, the elder bonded with a fourteen-year-old. No doubt the board member forgot the incident by the next day, but Rod treasures this memory, and today he produces Christian television to touch millions. The next act of family good will and humor you show to a child at church could win her heart and eventually bless multitudes. That's supporting the ministry of your church.

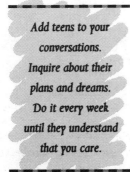

Add teens to your conversations. Inquire about their plans and dreams. Do it every week until they understand that you care.

Look for ways to build family trust and belonging. If your habit has been to speak to a few adults before and after services, expand that routine. Add teens to your conversations. Inquire about their plans and dreams. Do it every week until they come to understand that you care. Add a few teens and their needs to your prayer list. God may even give you a couple to mentor. The church young people need adult affirmation and acceptance. Now go a step further. Learn the names of several of the children.

Jake Kats, a church elder, always carried wrapped penny candy in a suit pocket. Every Sunday, he would bend low to speak to the children—even preschoolers—and sneak a piece of candy into their hands. Parents who frowned on sugar treats smiled at the attention this respected leader gave their four-year-olds. A wink, a sentence of praise, or a quick shoulder hug can produce wonders in a youth's heart. With God's help, you can support your church and pastor by creating nostalgic church-family memories that will endure in many lives.

Nostalgic Worship Memories
Singer Susie Luchsinger tells her Warm Church Memory:

> A warm church memory for me was when I was about five years old and my grandma would take me to church. It was a little bitty church of

about fifteen people. They would ask for requests, and I was always the first one to say number 462. My favorite song was "When the Roll Is Called up Yonder I'll Be There."

When I was twelve years old I gave my heart to the Lord, and I praise God that I have the assurance that I will be there to glorify him.

Susie's musical career began in church, requesting hymns as soon as she knew the numbers and later performing. For worship to nurture nostalgic bonding, there must be more than observation. Participation is essential. "Let the words of Christ, in all their richness, live in your hearts and make you wise. Use his words to teach and counsel each other. Sing Psalms and hymns and spiritual songs to the Lord with thankful hearts" (Ephesians 5:18–20). This worship teaching and singing is to have a participatory quality to it.

If your eight-year-old son or daughter is taking piano lessons, ask permission for a piano solo in children's church, youth club, or even a church service. Your youngster will treasure those two minutes to the end of his or her life. If you serve on the worship committee, look for cross-generational involvement.

As an eighth grader, I was asked to play my first trombone solo in a Sunday night church service. My family listened to me practice "Praise Him, Praise Him" until they couldn't tolerate it one more time. The bulletin scheduled me to play immediately after the offering. Of the thousands of Christian musical pieces available, the organist chose for the offertory, "Praise Him, Praise Him." For several moments there was panic in my soul. A perfectly arranged service would never have the same hymn twice in a row.

Then Jesus whispered that he would count a double "Praise Him" as a double honor that night. My solo went as well as an eighth-grader's solo might be expected. But from that night on I felt ownership in the life and worship of the church. From that moment on, I didn't go to church, I was the church. Susie understands that.

In many churches, cross-generational worship participation is offered through greeting teams, candle lighting, receiving the offering, platform singing with the worship team, Scripture readings, and drama vignettes. At any age you can find delight in wholehearted involvement in the movements of worship.

Nostalgia for church almost always involves music. Worship was one expression of love Jesus longed to see renewed in the Ephesian church.

> *I have so many warm church memories, but one of my favorites was when I was nine years old. I was attending our family church, a Reformed Episcopal Church in Baltimore. Every Sunday I wore white gloves, white patent leather shoes, and a frilly dress. To kneel on those kneelers in church was such a special treat, especially after I read that Psalm as a nine-year-old, "Oh come let us worship and bow down, let us kneel before the Lord our maker." Kneeling up to that point always hurt my knees. From then on it did wonders for my heart.*
>
> —Joni Erickson Tada

Counselor, author, and media personality Frank Minirth has warm church memories of worship:

One of my best memories is growing up in a little country church. It was white with trees all around it, and on Monday afternoon we'd play softball. On Sunday morning we'd sing the old

hymns of the faith. Of all the books that
have affected my life, in the top five would be
the old hymnbook. I can still remember word
for word those songs we'd sing Sunday after
Sunday: "I'm Resolved," "Never Alone,"
"Footsteps of Jesus"—they all still echo in my
mind. What wonderful memories they still
bring back.

I can still be moved to tears by the praise music I
enjoyed as a teen. I can still get excited over a '57
Chevy, too. But the '50s aren't about to return to
cars or church life. So I move on, enjoy a modern
front-wheel-drive car, and worship Christ from my
heart with contemporary church music. The worship
team, with singers, band, and frequent prayers, now
provides some of the most movingly spiritual worship times of my life. I participate with my voice
and hands raised, my prayers and tears. If this does
not come naturally to you, let it come deliberately.
Prepare your heart for worship Saturday night with
confession and longing for the presence of God. Sunday morning, hum your way through getting ready
for church. Turn off the news and sports and listen to
Christian radio or a worship CD on the way to church.

My longing for my church is that a decade or two
from now we'll look back on these days as precious
and powerful in worship. That's why *with God's help, I
promise to support the worship ministry of my church and
pastor.* I'll prepare my heart for worship, and participate emotionally and spiritually. I'll encourage those
who lead worship and I'll help a younger generation
find participatory roles and ownership as together
we worship our God and Savior.

Nostalgic Conversion Memories
Support your church in the evangelistic process of
providing a path to Jesus. With some churches this

involves an instruction class, for others a revival meeting; for some it's an altar call, for others there are private opportunities. I was raised in a rural setting, where there were paths to neighboring houses, paths to the "cricks," paths to the ponds and woods. When these paths were not used for a few months, they grew over with weeds and were lost from view. The paths in your church to a conversion experience with Jesus Christ must be well traveled. "Stand at the crossroads and look; ask for the ancient paths, ask where the good way is, and walk in it, and you will find rest for your souls" (Jeremiah 6:16, NIV).

Your role may be to bring people to the path, to encourage them to walk to Jesus, to pray for them on the path. Lee Strobel's wife brought him to the beginning of the path:

> *Sunday morning I was on a radio program, and in the afternoons I rode horses. On a particular day, it was as though an invisible hand reached out and touched me, and I found myself on the back row of the church as Dr. Louis Evans was speaking.*
> *Because I smelled like a horse, I didn't want to meet anyone, so I slipped out early. But I came back again and again. In the process I fell in love with Jesus, and he changed my life, and I've been increasingly in love with him for 50 years.*
> —Bill Bright, founder of Campus Crusade for Christ

My fondest memory happened on January 20, 1980. I was an atheist, and my wife had become a Christian through the influence of a church called Willowcreek that was meeting in a movie theater. She brought me to church that time. That particular day was the first time I'd been in church in years. I'd rejected Christ as a youngster. I sat there in the movie theater, and it was the first time in my life that I understood the message of Jesus Christ. As I drank it in and thought about it, I walked out saying two things. First, I didn't believe it was true. I wasn't ready at that point to repent of my sins and come to Christ as the forgiver of my sins and leader of my life. But secondly, I said, "If this is true, it has incredible implications for my life." Because of that day, January 20, 1980, I spent two years systematically using my journalistic and legal background to investigate: "Is there credibility to Christianity?" After doing that for two years and seeing the mountain of evidence that Jesus Christ was who he claimed to be, on November 8, 1981, I did receive Christ as the forgiver of my sins and leader of my life.

Help your neighbor find the path. My parents were utterly heathen at my birth. But when I was a month old, a neighbor invited my brother to ride the bus to Vacation Bible School. My mother was ecstatic at the thought of getting my eight-year-old brother out of the house for half a day. This was an opportunity for free baby-sitting. Bob went to VBS, and afterward someone from the church came to our house to invite all the family to Sunday school. From this neighborly invitation, my parents and older brother were soon converted to Christ.

The epistles of Paul tell and retell his conversion testimony. He never wearied of sharing how Jesus appeared to him and changed him from persecutor of Christians to messenger of Christ. His lifetime remembrance was: "I persecuted the church of God. But whatever I am now, it is all because God poured out his special favor on me" (1 Corinthians 15:9–10). Paul's path to Jesus led to his lifetime commitment to the church.

Your conversion path should include an opportunity for confession or declaration. All major events, whether marriage or buying a home, include times for public commitment or stating vows. Forms for this vary in the church, but baptism is still the most common:

> *A warm church memory for me is the night as a ten-and-a-half-year-old I came to Jesus as my Savior. The warmest part of the memory is the great loving arms embrace of one of the elders of the church, a man of nearly seventy years of age, who, when I knelt at the altar, put his arms around me, a ten-year-old boy, and told me how I could know Jesus.*
> —Jack Hayford, author and pastor

When I was twelve, it was time to be baptized. My memory is that I decided to sing my testimony. They baptized me, and I was dripping wet and shivering and singing, "I Don't Have to Wait Until I'm Grown Up." It was the first solo I sang, and I knew my father would be so proud of me. And my heavenly Father was looking down as well.
—Valerie Bell, author and singer

Have you declared your faith to your confirmation class, to the new believer's class, to the elders, or to the entire church? If you don't know how or where to do so, ask your pastor or a respected leader how you can confess your faith in Jesus Christ. You can support the ministry of your church and pastor in walking the path to Jesus. Then you can pledge, *With God's help, I promise to support the ministry of my church and pastor by bringing many along the path to Jesus.*

Nostalgic Pastor Memories
Pastors are God's called and appointed leaders, who

deserve our respect. When our nation goes to war, our president or prime minister will receive the support of both government and the masses. Our pastors are on the front line of spiritual war every day and must have our assistance.

> I've been a pastor for 44 years, but a warm church memory has to do with my background as a little boy in Finley, Tennessee. We had only one paved road in our town. It was hard to travel in the winter or the rainy season. We didn't have our own pastor, but ministers came from distant cities up to 75 miles away. They came when they could get there. The rest of the time my mother played piano and we had Sunday school. But those were wonderful days, and when the preachers did get to come, they were the greatest people in my life. Those were the days before television and famous sports figures. So my heroes were pastors, and my heart is warmed and thrilled with the memory of the great preachers of God who have been such a blessing and influence to me over the years. They are still my heroes, and I wish they were the heroes of the young people of America today."
> —Dr. L. H. Harwick, *Christ's Church, Nashville*

Young Harwick was more Christian in attitude than he knew at the time. Of pastors and elders we are taught to "hold them in the highest regard in love because of their work" (1 Thessalonians 5:13, NIV). Dr. Harwick's mother played the piano in church. The unspoken testimony is that this lady never badmouthed these preachers but spoke admirably of them in the presence of her son.

Giving honor to an office or person of office is not in vogue today. Jay Leno of *The Tonight Show* grows wealthy ridiculing America's president, along with every other international leader, whether political, judicial, business, or spiritual. Contempt is in, and honor is out. But I urge you to promise to *support* the ministry of your pastor, with God's help.

We need to honor our pastors so their practical needs are met. Bishop Samuel Green of St. John's Church of God in Christ tells this story:

> *Just as those who work underground to replace Cuba's government want to replace Castro, so the spiritual underground seeking the ruin of the church wants to remove the pastors.*

A warm church memory of one of my church members is that when I first started pastoring, a lady—in spite of the fact that I had a wife and seven children—took us in her home and fed us religiously every Sunday. She showed a Christian heart toward us. She was a beautiful Christian lady in the Lord.

The church is under spiritual attack, and that means the pastor is too. Just as those who work underground to replace Cuba's government want to replace Castro, so the spiritual underground seeking the ruin of the church wants to remove the pastors. Tactics to accomplish that goal are ingeniously numerous. Breaking down the pastor's morals, integrity, and family is always high on the list. But the easiest route is to freeze the pastor out financially. You need to honor your pastor and church with your faithful tithes and offerings to the Lord.

I'm one of many who pray daily for a mighty spiritual awakening in the land. Along with holiness and a hunger for the Word, I'm looking for revival to bring a restoration of healthy giving habits for God's people. And I see it happening—not universally yet, but with a spotty excitement as men and women find joy in giving.

We church people tend to be overly quiet about giving. Praise times will be about God's guiding and healing. We need to find a comfort level, even an enthusiasm, in hearing from those who know the grace of giving. As a young man, I heard a saint say, "Since I increased my weekly check to the church and added support for two missionaries, I haven't had a car repair or medical expense. These had been eating me up financially." That short testimony was one of the most powerful sermons I ever heard on giving.

We need to honor our pastors with our lips, our prayers, and our support in times of crisis. One preacher humorously reported that he had four hundred active people in his church; two hundred active for him, and two hundred active against him. Randy Phillips of Promise Keepers has a more godly report:

> I have a warm memory of my church. Two months ago my senior pastor shared some pain and bared his heart on an area of criticism that had come his way. The church rallied around him, supported him, and honored him. We told him we were behind him. The church is becoming a church that is breaking down the barrier between laity and clergy. I see men and women who are willing to become part of the solution for the problems the clergy are facing.

I've been a preacher for thirty years, and I've been around preachers longer than that. They are still my heroes. I try to guard my mouth about the imperfections of the ministers I know. My pastor doesn't have to be perfect to have my prayers and endorsement.

You don't want roast pastor at your dinner table. It'll cause indigestion for everyone. Rather, do secret acts of kindness for your pastor. Send your pastor and spouse a gift certificate for a dinner out with a note of how much you love them. E-mail a thank you of how a sermon touched your life.

You don't want roast pastor at your dinner table. It'll cause indigestion for everyone.

My granddaughter, age seven at the time, sat in church and drew a picture of our pastor in the pulpit. (Grandma had a collection of colored markers in her purse for occasions like this.) Gini wrote over the top: "I love my pastor," and handed this to him at the door. Months later he showed me the picture. He treasured this and never took it out of his Bible.

I have nostalgic memories of Pastor Berry, who was gifted in leading the common man and woman to faith in Christ, of Pastor Miller whose preaching made this eleven-year-old thrilled to see Jesus in the book of Exodus for a year, of Pastor Stansfield who empowered me in ministry opportunities as a teen, and of Pastor Johnson who has been a wise counselor through all my adult life. Twenty years ago I vowed to never criticize my wife, but only love and support her. The picayune things that once annoyed have either dropped from her life or my observation. In either case, it was one of the top ten best decisions I ever made. In the same manner I've resolved to support my pastor and not criticize. When you adopt this approach, you'll be surprised at how wonderful pastor is—and your spouse too!

Nostalgic Restoration Memories

How a church handles difficult situations and troubled people will send three-dimensional photo memories to everyone in the church. These memories will either bring appreciation and awe, or drive people away. Always lean to the side of restoring the weak and not shooting the wounded. You may be the next wounded one.

Churches, like families, must provide a way back—a fresh start, forgiveness for the prodigal. Peter, who vowed eternal faithfulness to Jesus, publicly denied three times that he even knew the Lord. How would Jesus handle him the next time they met? Jesus forgave Peter, directing him in fresh opportunities to show his love and care for the church (John 21:15–17). When the woman caught in adultery was thrown at Jesus' feet, the Pharisees coldly were ready to stone her, but Jesus protected her, forgave her, and sent her on restored (John 8:1–11). Often, the further people fall, the deeper they will love. The greatest advocates for mercy are those who've known the hardness of their own transgressions. The finest counselors are those who've been through crises.

Bill Hybels of Willowcreek Church has a nostalgic restoration story to commemorate:

> One very warm church memory I have happened about a year ago when one of our vocalists, who had been a key part of our ministry for a very long time, had a difficulty in her marriage that wound up leading to the end of her marriage. We tried to work through it with her and the elders, and she wasn't able to work through it. She ran from God and ran from the church.

But a year later she came to her senses. She came back and confronted what it was that had gone awry. She humbled herself with repentance and reestablished respect and a relationship with the elders. One night she stood in front of our whole church and asked for forgiveness from the congregation. Grace was extended to her, and she was warmly received back into our congregation. She is using her spiritual gifts again with her vocal talent. It was a memorable picture of grace at work, of a life reclaimed. I'll never forget it the rest of my life.

There are nationwide, supposedly Christian, watchdog organizations whose only purpose is to accuse the brethren. Their accusations are consistently unresearched and destructive. God has clearly commanded, "Thou shalt not bear false witness against thy neighbor" (Exodus 20:16, KJV). Similar watchdog clubs can emerge within the church. Avoid listening to any gossip, refuse to repeat it, and look for words and ways to heal the hurts of life. Of Jesus we learn, "A bruised reed he will not break, and a smoldering wick he will not snuff out" (Matthew 12:20, NIV). Jesus always sought to restore health to the wounded and fan the fire where it had almost gone out in a person's life. Rather than denounce Judas, Jesus even protected the confidentiality of his traitor at the Last Supper.

Bring healing to the bruised and fire to those who are fading. Jesus wept often and compassionately. When he saw a city in spiritual ruin, he cried with anguish. The right response to a report of a brother or sister who has fallen is to hold the report lightly, for it may not be true; and if confirmed, to weep, pray, and be a healing, influencing friend. I have a friend in ministry who had developed some hurtful habits. I grieved for him, prayed for him, and took him out to lunch to confront the issue. The Lord turned this brother to the right direction that day and restored the health of his service. A bruised reed has healed, a smoldering wick is again burning brightly for Jesus.

Above all, seek to model a life that has been restored by the grace of God, for we are all fallen and dysfunctional in sin. But Christ has saved us.

It's the Heart

Support your church, participate in it so that you build warm church family memories, worship memories, conversion memories, pastoral leadership memories, and restoration memories. As with buggy whips and oil lamps, we'll loosen our grip on specific earlier forms of church life.

A warm church memory for me centers on the day I came out of the gay lifestyle and walked back into my church. I was afraid I'd find nothing but rejection from the people who knew what I'd been involved with. Instead, I found many Christians who did want to show a combination of compassion and conviction as they dealt with me. Some of the happiest words I ever heard as a Christian were "Joe, welcome back. We're glad to see you here."

—Joe

Every fall for decades, I went on hayrides. I'm nostalgic for hayrides. But much more than the farm tour, I have hayride memories of friendships, laughter, a little mischief, and singing God's praise. I'm nostalgic for the song "Since Jesus Came into My Heart." But more than the song, I have warm memories of the church full of the joy of praise in song. May God lead you and your church into forms of service and worship that will evoke nostalgia when you look back to this day. That's the test of greatness. May the glory of God pass from this generation to the next in your church.

I can live without ice cream from The Parlor. My favorite park and I have learned to survive without each other. But on one thing I can't compromise: I must have an authentically healthy church.

With God's help, I promise to support the ministry of my church and pastor.

That's a promise worth keeping by a person of promise.

Additional Warm Church Memories

"I have a wonderful memory of being a preschool boy who always enjoyed standing up on the pew beside my parents in this little church we attended. The feeling communicated was one of acceptance and joy just to worship together as a family."
—*Erwin Lutzer, Moody Church*

"I have a lot of warm church memories. I came from a family in which we were sevem days a week kind of Christians. When the church was open, we were always there. I loved Sunday school when I was a little girl. I loved the object lessons."
—*Elizabeth Elliott, author and missionary*

"At the very heart of your life should be a church. One of the best memories I can remember is in central Africa, after a mighty revival had taken place, opposing tribes had come together. To celebrate, we

had a Communion service. Here were men who had been eating one another's flesh now utterly transformed, breaking bread and drinking wine. I'll never forget two opposing men now in Christ coming to break the bread, pouring the wine and hugging each other. Africans never did that—hug each other and say, "I love you." I remember how the tears came up in my eyes as I saw the mighty grace of God demonstrated in what can take place in a heart. That was true revival. That was the warm memory I carried as a boy right through to this very hour."
—*Stephen Olford*

"When I think about a warm church memory in my life, I remember when I was 19 years old I was still in college, but I was going to spend a summer playing basketball in the Orient. My church had a special Steve Bell Day on one Sunday, and on that day they raised enough money for me to go, plus $800 to help others going on this mission trip. I appreciate my local church having vision for that kind of ministry. It made a major impact on my own life and my understanding of missions. I look back and think, if they could believe in me that much, it gives my heart joy as I think back on it."
—*Steve Bell, author*

"A warm church memory for me is the first time my four-year-old invited me to go to a little Holiness church in Monrovia, California. I was not a Christian, but I went there and got involved in a Sunday school class. This was the first time in my life that I was brought under the Word of God. It was there, studying the life of the apostle Paul, that I became convicted that I was a sinner and that I needed Christ as Savior. It was Galatians 2:20 that challenged me. Paul said that he was crucified with Christ, 'nevethe-

less I live, yet not I but Christ lives in me, and the life I now live in the flesh I live by the faith of the Son of God who loved me and gave himself for me.'"
—*John Spencer, author*

"A warm church memory for me is as a little boy sitting in a very small congregation in South America. My father was a businessman, and . . . we would sit around the Lord's Table with the bread and one cup, because that's the way we celebrated it. To see my father stand up, read Psalm 91 or another Psalm, and lead in Communion, and then pass the bread around and pass the cup: That's the youngest memory I have as a boy of our local church, and it still stays with me, and the Lord's Supper is still my favorite time in church."
—*Luis Palau, evangelist*

CHAPTER 6

Something in My Eye

*With God's help, I promise to identify and address
the hidden prejudices of my heart.*

Whenever the doctor prescribes drops for my eyes,
my wife threatens to call in the S. W. A. T. team if I
don't hold still and cooperate. She complains that
her nursing chore would be easier if I didn't squint
my eyelids with alligator-jaw force. I'd prefer to
cooperate, but every time I open one of my lids a
mere slit for a sneaky peek at the enemy's weapon,
I'm shot in the pupil with what feels like battery
acid. And that's only round one. The prescription is
for two drops—per eye. That means at least a four-
rounder.

Multiple sets of eyeglasses lie conveniently scattered
around our house, but nary a contact lens will be
found. I don't permit strange objects in my eye, and
any object absent at birth I consider strange. I even
know the day I started feeling this way.

I was playing eleven-year-old Little League baseball
when a bird, or maybe an overgrown gnat, chose my
eye for a landing zone. The actual species remains
undetermined, because whatever it was, I drowned
it and washed it away in a teary flood. My coach was
unsuccessful in his attempts to pry open my lid to
spy out the problem. He wanted me to stand in one
place for an on-the-field emergency operation, but I

was too clever for that. I wouldn't permit those fingers in my eye. Later in the day, when my eye had recovered, something in my heart still hurt. Try as I might to convince myself that I just didn't like fingers in my eye, it didn't work. I didn't want my coach's fingers in my eye because my coach was African-American.

Prejudice is blinding at any age. Mine caught me by surprise, because I didn't know I had it. My coach was a great man, and I enjoyed being around him. At some distance. Not too close. Certainly not finger-probing close. I despised myself, as shame rolled in like summer thunderheads. Don't you dare get soft on me and dismiss this as childish false guilt. In forty years I've never whispered this story to anyone, not a family member or friend. But I remember it as though it were yesterday. There had been hidden prejudice in my heart, just waiting for the opportunity to jump out and bite me.

Some prejudices are as blatant as the Aryan Nation and the Klu Klux Klan. Others operate so efficiently undercover that we forget they exist or deny their presence. Yet prejudice remains as destructive a force in fallen humanity as lust and greed. We don't wrestle with prejudice with the intensity or frequency we ascribe to lust and greed, because we don't see our partialities as a problem, and certainly not a sin. Our prejudices are hidden under the thin veneer of personal values, cultural stability, homogeneous churches, parental teaching, religious dogma, regional tradition, and convictions that "they really are all like that."

Although Jesus grew up in the small town of Nazareth, he never displayed the common provincial prejudices. In fact, Jesus was obviously intentional in demonstrating non-discriminatory deportment.

Jesus conducted his ministry with words and actions that challenged all the ingrained and accepted prejudices of his day. He saw fighting prejudice not as a political issue to avoid but a kingdom platform plank to boldly proclaim. When Jesus declared that his ministry was "to preach good news to the poor . . . proclaim freedom for the prisoners and recovery of sight for the blind, to release the oppressed" (Luke 4:18), he challenged prejudices and slapped the face of every traditional priest and prophet in the land.

> *Jesus conducted his ministry with words and actions that challenged all the ingrained and accepted prejudices of his day.*

When people today read his words about his ministry plan, they are likely to think, "How sweet. He was such a good man." But if Jesus came as a pastoral candidate to a church and said, "If you install me as your minister, I'll give most of my time to bringing God's good news to the poor in the low-income projects and to the homeless, to caring for the incarcerated in the county jail, to helping the physically and mentally handicapped find healing and wholeness, and to fighting the oppression of minorities who can't buy homes where they want or secure the jobs they've been trained for," how would the pulpit committee respond? Many would conclude that they would be wise to bypass Jesus and find a preacher less radical.

Christ's announcement of his goals was moment one. He continued "in your face" anti-prejudice tactics every day in his ministry. When he touched lepers, protected adulterers, ate with publicans, empowered women, received anointing by a harlot, and made Samaritan friends, Jesus was both loving people and declaring war on prejudice. That means that for you and me, confronting prejudice is a question of Christian authenticity. Or compromised authenticity. To be a genuine Christian is to fight discrimination, to uncover and address even the hidden prejudices of the heart. Are you prepared to do that, to affirm Christ's dreams for you and to address hidden and forgotten bigotry that has blinded you? If so, then open both eyes and mouth resolving, *With God's help, I promise to identify and address the hidden prejudices of my heart.*

Jesus on Racial Prejudice

Jesus had no eye problems when it came to racial and ethnic prejudices. He was clearsighted in his understanding that God loved the whole world and that his mission was to offer eternal life to whoever would believe in him (John 3:16). Jesus knew that God chose Abraham, not so that all the blessings of God would be spoils for his descendants but so that "all the families of the earth will be blessed through you" (Genesis 12:3). The Jewish people of Jesus' day had something in their eyes that blinded their vision regarding God's place for them in the world. They acted as religious misers, rather than missionaries of love to all nations. Jesus knew God had told Moses, "All the earth belongs to me. And you will be to me a kingdom of priests" (Exodus 19:5–6). God elected the Hebrews to be ministers to all the earth, missionaries to the world he loves.

Jesus often quoted Isaiah, who prophesied, "You will be a light to guide all nations to me" (Isaiah 42:6), and "I will make you a light to the Gentiles, and you will bring my salvation to the ends of the earth" (Isaiah 49:6). Jesus was the Son of God, the God who loved the city Nineveh, even when the prophet Jonah didn't. Jesus was a student of Daniel, who functioned as a captive missionary prophet in a foreign country. Jesus read Ezekiel and Jeremiah's writings to Gentile nations. The love of God for each and every man, woman, and child permeated Jesus' soul, eliminating prejudice from his heart and discrimination from his conduct.

Jesus' religious opponents frequently attempted to trap him by asking questions they felt were beyond answers or might lead to conflict with establishment positions. One religious law expert quoted Moses to Jesus: "You must love the Lord your God with all your heart, all your soul, all your strength, and all your mind. And love your neighbor as yourself." He might have heard that Jesus publicly rejected the accepted ethic, "Love your neighbor and hate your enemy" (Matthew 5:43). The challenger's question was "Who is my neighbor?" (Luke 10:27–29).

> *The Jewish leaders had raised hating your enemy to religious duty, and "enemy" was permeated with nationalistic racial overtones.*

The "hate your enemy" phrase was an addition and perversion to what Moses taught in the law. This was not a trivial pursuit kind of dispute. Hatred for enemies and those unlike oneself had been elevated to duty and art. James Stalker wrote, "It is well known how the Jews actually did hate the Samaritans." And this racial hatred was a worldwide practice. "Among both the Greeks and Romans it was esteemed, as is remarked in *Ecce Homo*, the highest praise of a dead man to say that none had done more good to his friends or more harm to his foes."[1] The Jewish leaders had raised hating your enemy to religious duty, and "enemy" was permeated with nationalistic racial overtones. The leader who asked, "Who is my neighbor?" expected *neighbor* to have a limited scope, carrying with it an endorsement for prejudiced racial hatred. Jesus answered by narrating the story of the good Samaritan. A Jewish man was mugged, beaten, robbed, and left for dead beside the road. A priest and a Levite temple assistant encountered the scene and walked right past, not lifting a finger to aid the desperate traveler. A Samaritan gentleman saw the Jewish man and "felt deep pity. Kneeling beside him, the Samaritan soothed his wounds with medicine and bandaged them. Then he put the man on his own donkey and took him to an inn, where he took care of him. The next day he gave the innkeeper two pieces of silver," with a promise to pay more if the bill ran higher (Luke 10:32–35).

The Samaritan was declared to be the neighbor to the Jewish man. With this story Jesus simultaneously eliminated hating enemies, outlawed racial prejudice between Jews and Samaritans, and redefined *neighbor*. We still tend to think of neighbors as other people. Jesus defined neighbors not as the people to be loved but as the heart of the person who loves. "Now go and do the same," he instructed (Luke 10:37).

The question isn't whether Africans, Anglos, Asians, Europeans, Hispanics, and Native Americans are your neighbors. The question is, "Are you a loving neighbor to them, or are you holding prejudicial attitudes toward others?"

Jesus "walked the talk" by intentionally making Samaritan friends. Samaria separated Judea and Galilee in geography, and it was customary for Jews to take the bypass route around this region, even though it made the trip longer. On a mission trip that broke all the discriminatory travel rules, Jesus went into Samaria, visited with the people, made lasting friends and plenty of followers (John 4:1ff).

The old saying "Love your neighbor and hate your enemy" diabolically made racial prejudice not only acceptable but an ethical good. These prejudices caused suspicious ill will within communities and wars between states. The Romans ruled Judea. Loving your neighbors and enemies meant showing kindness and intentionally welcoming both Samaritans and Romans into their lives. Most Jews had no such intention.

> *If lust has slain thousands, then greed has killed tens of thousands, and prejudice has slaughtered millions upon millions.*

We need to confront this hidden truth: If lust has slain thousands, then greed has killed tens of thousands, and prejudice has slaughtered millions upon millions.

Thirty to one hundred million Africans were captured, transported, and sold as slaves. (If you're Caucasian, read that sentence again and let the horror of it begin to touch you.)

World War II was a war of prejudice. The Nazis judged white Germans as superior to all other humans, and thus endowed with the right to rule and kill. Jews were to be exterminated.

In the Rwandan war of the early '90s, millions were hacked to death in crude, brutal fashion. What motivation generated this slaughter? It wasn't sexual lust. Greed was there in some measure. But the heart of the issue was multigenerational prejudice between the Tutsi and Hutu tribes. A distinguishing physical feature is that the members of one tribe typically grow taller than the other. Warriors often selected their victims based on nothing more than height.

The Chicago Tribune published a multipanel cartoon depicting a military general bragging, "Yes, I've killed Bosnians. Yes, I've killed Serbians. Yes, I've killed Albanians. I'm a nondiscriminatory killer." The humor is thin—this was a political cartoon. Wars in this part of the world are expressions of prejudice, the view that people who differ from my kind don't share equally with me rights to prosperity and protection, or even land, and liberty, and life itself.

Discrimination has been defined as the unequal treatment of equals. Discrimination is expressed in overt behavior, while prejudice is the attitude of the heart. My two children, Larry and Amy, are both adopted Koreans. During their school years they were called "Chink" and "Nigger." Those who experience discrimination daily won't be impressed, but it was a taste. The distaste of prejudice, like smog in the air, is ever present. A black driver and I pulled away from a stoplight at the same time and speed. The bright flashing lights of the police sedan startled me.

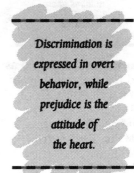

Discrimination is expressed in overt behavior, while prejudice is the attitude of the heart.

Two months later, I'm still startled that the driver of color was the one pulled over. (No Latino or African-American is startled by this account.) I assume he was ticketed for some minor infraction, but I wonder if the real issue was local police racial harassment. If I see it happen again, I've vowed to pull over, get the facts, and report them as widely as I can.

The University of Illinois is under attack for the continued employ of the fake Chief Illiniwek as its school mascot. At every major event the chief does a war dance routine to stir the passions of the fans. It also stirs the passions of Native Americans, who feel demeaned. Chicago columnist Mike Imrem, a University of Illinois alumnus and longtime defender of the chief, is beginning to see the light: "It's insulting for them [advocates of the mascot] to say Indians—the Illini tribe and others—shouldn't be insulted because Chief Illiniwek glorifies them. Who in the world are we to tell anybody when their culture is or isn't being insulted? The implication from those sympathetic to the chief is that Indians just don't get it. The truth is, the University of Illinois just hasn't gotten it."[2]

Mike has gotten it. He uncovered and addressed a hidden prejudice in his heart.

Prejudicial attitudes that fuel most of the world's wars can still lurk in the hearts of those who call themselves Christians. The prejudices that launch armed conflicts are close relatives to the prejudices that segregate churches and Christian schools, divide the body of Christ, and cause us to treat many in a non-Christ-like manner. So we need to make this promise: *With God's help, I promise to identify and address the hidden prejudices of my heart.*

The worst racial prejudice of the ancient world was between Jews and Gentiles, who were separated even in worship by a dividing wall of hostility. This wall was physical—in the temple—and emotional—in the heart—like the Berlin Wall that divied Communist east from democratic west physically and emotionally. But the apostle Paul shouted in victory that "Christ himself has made peace between Jews and Gentiles by making us all one people. He has broken down the wall of hostility that used to separate us" (Ephesians 2:14).

So overwhelming was the annihilation of racism in the church that it was almost too much for people to comprehend. It was a mysterious matter that those they discriminated against must now be received and loved as brothers and sisters. What is the mystery? "This mystery is that through the gospel the Gentiles are heirs together with Israel, members of one body" (Ephesians 3:6).

> "Christ himself has made peace . . . by making us all one people. He has broken down the wall of hostility that used to separate us."
> —Ephesians 2:14

Ron Sider concludes. "Ultimately, racism in the church is a denial of the Gospel. It is a heretical, disobedient rejection of God's purpose in Christ, which is why Paul publicly rebuked Peter for racial bias, condemning Peter for 'not acting in line with the truth of the Gospel.' Racial reconciliation in the church is a visible demonstration of the Gospel."[3]

The boy who didn't want to be touched by a black coach now is a member of a racially integrated church. He has a long way to go, but he shows progress. One of our pastors is black, as is our youth pastor. My covenant group leader who puts his arm around me and prays for me is African-American. Although this dear friend has an earned doctorate and is a research scientist, he is currently unemployed. Racial discrimination is hard to prove, but it is a hill for him to climb over in any job search. Our youth group is a beautiful rainbow union of colors and cultures. In heaven they will be comfortable worshipping the Lamb of God at his throne with those from every nation, tribe, people, and language (Revelation 7:9). For me, fellowship is greater and worship is more pure in this church without walls.

Live as a person of promise and resolve, *With God's help, I promise to identify and address the hidden racial prejudices of my heart.*

Jesus on Gender Prejudice

Jesus had 20/20 vision when it came to gender issues. Wealthy women economically supported Jesus and his team as they conducted their mission (Luke 8:3). Jesus empowered women, defended them, and fellowshipped with them as equals (John 8:1–11; Luke 10:38–41). Our Lord's first appearance after his resurrection was to a woman whose mission was to go and convince the fearful and doubting men (Matthew 28:9–10). That whole account destroys the myth of male courage and strength. God's first message that opened the Christian era was to young Mary about a child who was to be called the Son of the Most High (Luke 1:32). It wasn't to a male preacher-prophet but to a godly teen girl that the Lord entrusted this news. So with the two most significant events in history, the birth and the resurrection of Jesus, God gave primary leadership roles to two women.

On the trip into Samaria, Jesus decided to make it a two-for-one package. He would not only confront racial prejudices but also make a special friendship with a woman who had an unsavory history. The disciples were prejudiced against the Samaritans, yet "they were astonished to find him talking to a woman" (John 4:27). These men were more prejudiced against women than against Samaritans and other gentiles they considered unclean. The disciples were slow in realizing that Jesus disdainfully brushed aside gender prejudices.

While gender prejudices can be hurtful to others, they can also be harmful to one's self. Pontius Pilate's wife "sent him this message: 'Leave this innocent man alone, because I had a terrible nightmare about him last night'" (Matthew 27:19). Pilate arrogantly ignored her, signed Jesus' death warrant, and sealed his own cowardly renown.

Through the years God has been patiently peeling off cataract layers of hidden but blinding gender prejudices. My wife has been lovingly patient and to her credit has learned to assert herself, to find her own place, power, and position.

Early in our marriage, I overtly attempted to influence her hair and clothing styles with my strong preferences. That's straight-out suffocating and degrading prejudice. Now my daughter styles my hair, and Nancy picks out my ties. The truth is, I'm style challenged and colorblind! Colorblindness is one of God's practical jokes to humble my arrogance: "Sweetheart, I've forgotten—will one of these ties work with this sweater?" I'm reduced to childlike submission before I can leave the house in the morning.

I once saw my role as the family decision-maker. Period. Now I seek to be a gentle servant leader and big-time family cheerleader. In earlier years, I laughed at sexist jokes. Now I find them disgusting. Earlier, I needed to be better than my wife in education and career. Now I support Nancy in all her dreams and want her to maximize every talent and spiritual gift God has given her. She's outdistanced me in education, and her design career is in high gear.

To peel off layers of hidden gender prejudices is not to become unisex or undo biblical roles. There are wonderful differences between Nancy and me that make us complementary rather than redundant, mutually attractive rather than boring. But to hire a woman because you can pay her less is a prejudice and injustice that needs to end. When women have difficulty entertaining clients in traditional fishing and golf outings, it arises from discrimination based on prejudicial "old boy networks."

Women can be sexist, too. When *all* men are judged to be insensitive, power intoxicated, sports addicted, and car crazy, it can't be the truth, can it?

> *When all men are judged to be insensitive, power intoxicated, sports addicted, and car crazy, it can't be the truth, can it?*

I haven't arrived, but I think I'm climbing. Will you join me? A person of promise answers, *With God's help, I promise to identify and address the hidden gender prejudices of my heart.*

Jesus on Class Prejudice

Jesus welcomed into his life all the personalities that would raise the eyebrows and curl the lips of the prejudiced within the ranks. Simon the Pharisee thought he was already on the edge of propriety when he invited Jesus as a guest to his home. *My Pharisee friends will give me a tongue lashing after they hear about this,* he thought. The hope of keeping this meal a secret vanished. The gossip chain activated the moment Jesus entered the home. Before the formal meal was served, a crowd had gathered. One woman with a sinful reputation was bold enough to crash the party and come directly to Jesus. What an unseemly mess! She was prostrate and weeping.

Tears of remorse dripped off her cheeks onto Jesus' feet. Embarrassed, she wiped the tears with her hair. Then she kissed Jesus' feet and anointed them with an expensive perfume.

Simon had never been part of such a disgusting display. His estimation of Jesus dropped like a stock market crash. "He said to himself, 'This proves that Jesus is no prophet. If God had really sent him, he would know what kind of woman is touching him. She's a sinner!'" (Luke 7:39). Jesus proved himself more than a prophet by answering Simon's thoughts. Jesus rebuked Simon, because when he welcomed Jesus into his home, Simon hadn't extended him the minimum courtesy of the Eastern traditional embrace and kiss.

Jesus also told Simon a story in which two people's debts were forgiven; the one forgiven the biggest debt was the most loving and grateful. Then Jesus turned to the woman and said, "Your sins are forgiven" (Luke 7:48).

Simon couldn't welcome people into his home or church whom he judged (prejudged) were beneath him. He was an economic and moral snob, blind to the beauty of diversity. Christ is determined to eradicate such social prejudice from his church. It's a matter of authenticity. "It doesn't matter if you are a Jew or a Gentile, circumcised or uncircumcised, barbaric, uncivilized, slave, or free. Christ is all that matters and he lives in all of us" (Colossians 3:11).

There are gnats of prejudice in eyes that blind us to the value in those dissimilar for any number of reasons. A church that dedicated their new building invited me as guest speaker for a special event. I inquired about their youth ministries and was told that these were now limited to church families.

They had ceased welcoming children from the neighborhood because they left fingerprints on their new walls. I concluded that they now worshipped their new building and had forsaken the gospel.

> Suppose someone comes into your meeting dressed in fancy clothes and expensive jewelry, and another comes in who is poor and dressed in shabby clothes. If you give special attention and a good seat to the rich person, but say to the poor one, "You can stand over there, or else sit on the floor"—well, doesn't this discrimination show that you are guided by wrong motives? (James 2:3)

Remember, discrimination is the overt conduct that comes from a heart of prejudice. An authentic Christian or church makes anyone that Christ loves feel welcome and wanted.

A person of compromise assigns people to differing classes, leading to the common eye problem of "looking down" on others. A person of promise has corrected vision, affirming, *With God's help, I promise to identify and address the hidden social prejudices of my heart.*

Jesus on Denominational Barriers
Jesus took his disciple-staff to a Gentile city, Caesarea Philippi, to declare, "I will build my church" (Matthew 16:18). He always spoke of his church as singular, and he prayed for its unity. Ron Sider put it in this vernacular: "Jesus established one church, not a shopping mall of denominations."[4]

God has been steadily uncovering and addressing blinding prejudices in my life for decades. If my Savior is to deal with them all, I may be a long drain on the American Social Security system. Those who know me best would affirm that I was once a denominational snob. I carried prejudices about every denomination except my own, and I didn't like that one much either. I was a labeler. I wanted to know what schools you graduated from and what denomination you belonged to so I could pigeon-hole you. I had dozens of categories, and each denomination fit one of these classifications. It was inconvenient to actually know a person, because if this person didn't conform to my prejudices, I had a problem.

God gave me many such problems, and I began to see him working in people and churches outside of my filing system. "Lord, you can't work over there. My label on them doesn't provide for that." I should have known better. For some reason, my parents did not appreciate it when I told them what they could or could not do. "You can't see the principal; I for-bid it" or "You can't use the car tonight; I'm using it" didn't go over very well. Why, then, did I think I had a right to dictate to God where his Spirit might abide and work? "The wind blows wherever it pleas-es," Jesus said (John 3:8), and he was speaking of the Holy Spirit.

God's Spirit is working in his one great church, and most of us are putting up our sails to catch his wind and not be left behind. From Promise Keepers to Prayer and Fasting to PADS, Christ's great church is revealing itself as one body with many parts, all learning to stride forward with athletic grace. With increasing conviction, people of promise resolve: *With God's help, I promise to identify and address the hidden denominational prejudices of my heart.*

Taking off the Blinders
We all have eye problems. I couldn't see with the gnat in my eye, and I didn't want to see my coach's fingers in my eye. My parents raised me to be non-

prejudicial; yet year by year I discover hidden prejudices that God and his Word insist I must overcome. Where have these prejudices been hiding? I think I know the answer. They haven't been hiding. I've been wearing blinders.

John M. Perkins, founder of the Christian Community Development Association, writes:

> Overt racism is gradually disappearing, but a subtle lethal strain of the disease remains. . . . We call it passive racism. . . . Passive racism is a way of looking at the world that is much like wearing racial blinders—not bothering to see and understand the effects of race because we don't have to in order to survive. Blinders are ingenious. By limiting a horse's peripheral vision, the horse forges forward in the only direction it can see. . . . But even if the horse cannot see this other world, it still exists—full of dangers, difficulties, opportunities. The horse is just unconscious of it.[5]

God is taking off the prejudicial blinders from his children. Lingering racial superiority, gender insensitivity, cultural cocooning, and denominational walls have survived quietly within our structures. Some of these blinders have been passed down from generation to generation. The first step in taking off the blinders is not to fight with God's hand when he says, "It's time to take off the blinders." My sexist and denominational blinders made life simple. They also made life stupid, miserable, unproductive, and painful. God tugged at my blinders, and I pushed his hand away. I didn't want to complicate my life by seeing the world in a new way.

What can we do with these blinders? I can offer a few suggestions from my own life experience:

• When the Lord takes off your blinders, look around. For instance, a few days ago I spent two hours looking over the cultural and African-American literature sections of our Barnes and Noble Bookstore. I looked for literature that told the story, even the pain, of being a minority in my land. I skimmed several books and bought three.

• Be intentionally crosscultural with your church and relationships. Make at least one friend or prayer partner of another culture or race. It may take awhile for trust to build. Be trustworthy with a servant-friend attitude, not a caseworker mentality.

• Savor new ideas, stories, accents, personalities, and viewpoints as you would savor a lakeside sunrise with deer on the shore. My life is immeasurably richer since God began removing my blinders and expanding my horizon.

• If you live in the suburbs, read the city section of the newspaper. If you live in the city, read the news of other regions. Run for the school board and address racial issues. Volunteer for the police review board and listen to the community cultural problems. And always "think of others as better than yourself" (Philippians 2:3).

With God's help, I promise to identify and address the hidden prejudices of my heart.

That's a promise worth keeping by people of promise.

"Prejudice has many faces. Some faces look evil. Others just look idiotic because prejudice is a pre-conceived idea rather than logical conclusion."
—*Author unknown*

"Racism has always been obsolete in that it has no legitimate use in civil society. The problem is getting people to recognize that it's obsolete."
—*Thurgood Marshall, U. S. Supreme Court Justice*

"Many Hispanics wonder what good there is in join-ing a black/white dialogue that was begun in 1776 and was vigorously resurrected in the 1960s—but is still nowhere close to being resolved."
—*Jesse Miranda*

"One sign and wonder, biblically speaking, that alone can prove the power of the gospel is that of reconciliation"
—*Vinay Samuel, Indian theologian*

CHAPTER 7

To the Worlds with Love

*With God's help, I promise to influence
my world with the love of Christ.*

The local news told of a six-year-old girl found
starved to death with five broken ribs in her home.
Three adults, including a parent, are being charged
with second degree murder. It's my custom to pray
for the living, but my heart cried out: Dear Jesus,
receive this child and comfort her with your love,
which she never tasted in her world down here. And
help me bring your love to someone's world today.

The love of Jesus, God's Son, the Lord of Glory, is so
high and holy that I tremble lest I desecrate it with
common words. The love of Jesus, the Bright and
Morning Star, the Sun of Righteousness, the Light of
the World, must not be marred or dimmed by my
simple thoughts. The love of the Good Shepherd,
our Refuge and Strength, our Helper and Healer, the
Friend of Sinners, is sympathetic beyond my testimony and stories. The love of our Passover, the Sin
Bearer, the Crucified and Risen Savior, cost him
more than anyone can imagine or speak. The love of
the Hope of Glory, the Way, the Truth, and the Life,
the Mansion Builder, will yet surpass anything we
have tasted to this day.

This is the love we are to take to our worlds.

Two Kinds of Worlds

For God so loved the *world* that he gave his one and only Son, so that everyone who believes in him will not perish but have eternal life.
—*John 3:16, italics added*

O Lord my God, when I in awesome wonder, consider all the *worlds* thy hands have made.
—*Carl Boberg, "How Great Thou Art," italics added*

There you have the two perspectives: God sees the world and loves it, but we see many worlds, many places and peoples. The one world that God loves includes the many worlds that we must influence with the love of Jesus.

There are the worlds we know so well—the world of our family circle, the world of the neighborhood in which we live, the world of a familiar workplace. There are also lesser-known worlds that we bump up against—worlds of commerce and culture, politics and prisons. Then there are worlds awaiting our discovery—worlds of immigrants, of the persecuted, of the perishing. Without the love of Jesus any world is an inhospitable desert. A world with the love of Jesus is an oasis for the heart.

The Community World

The wheelbarrow was parked in front of the Royal Center post office. On his morning round, Everett often purchased a few groceries before he pushed and wheeled his way one mile back home. Bent horizontally at the waist and wearing old ragged clothing, Everett was a familiar town landmark, along with a few barns and vaneless windmills. He seemed more a part of the landscape than a person.

Everett had lived in Royal Center all his life, except for those war years. Some in town remembered that before the war he had been a young, respected school teacher. Shattered by the atrocities, he returned from the conflict to live with his mother. Humanity's inhumanities made him unemployably peculiar, socially and emotionally a plum-bob off center. He was the town hermit, surviving on a small lot with a Social Security disability check, five cows, chickens, and twice as many cats. Years before, his mother had died, leaving Everett alone.

With broken windows, caved-in roof, and unmowed grass, Everett's only neighborhood protection was that the house appeared more haunted than habitable. The house leaked in the rain and slowly began to collapse around him. He and his feline menagerie were reduced to occupying one corner of one room while chickens scratched in the abandoned areas. The winter heat source was a wood-burning stove that Everett stoked every night. With the fire exhausted by morning, the inside and outside temperatures were nearly the same. February mornings at sub-zero Fahrenheit were common, before wind-chill subtractions.

> *What would Jesus do? Would he love this nearly naked and homeless man? Would he help and heal a person not in his right mind?*

A new preacher in town wondered why no one tried to help this neighbor. He soon learned that the local culture was to not stick one's nose into the affairs of others unless invited, and even then reluctantly and cautiously. Everett had never asked for any kind of assistance, so "live and let live" ruled. Except that the preacher feared Everett wouldn't survive one more hard winter when the creek froze deep and the snow blew inside.

What would Jesus do? Would he love this nearly
naked and homeless man? Would he help and heal a
person not in his right mind? Would he taste the
suffering of someone in the community?

As Jesus stepped out of a boat, he met a man possessed of many demons. "Homeless and naked, he
had lived in a cemetery for a long time. As soon as
he saw Jesus, he shrieked and fell to the ground
before him, screaming, 'Why are you bothering me,
Jesus?'" (Luke 8:28). Jesus talked to the man, learned
his name, and felt sympathy for him over his
oppression. Hadn't the Son of God already declared
that he came to set the captive free? (Luke 4:18).
Even without a request for help, Jesus ordered the
demons out of the man. The love in Christ's heart
for this demented man was request enough. In short
order the town and surrounding countryside "saw
the man who had been possessed by demons sitting
quietly at Jesus' feet, clothed and sane" (Luke 8:35).

The Royal Center preacher saw a man who was in no
better shape than the demon-possessed chap Jesus
liberated. On his first visit the preacher rapped on
the door, being careful not to knock it down. A
timid or fearful voice called out, "Who's there?"

"The preacher," he sang out, "may I come in?" God's
servant stepped inside. Nearly overcome by the
stench, he followed the voice and the cats to
Everett. From his bed Ev sat up to meet his first
guest in years. The preacher asked about his health,
his firewood, and school teaching memories. He
also spoke to Everett of God's love and of the Savior,
Jesus. The preacher sensed heart, mind, personality,
and faith responding, stirring from decades of slum-
ber. They even prayed together, with Everett speaking to Jesus like a child. The preacher visited his
new friend often, bringing food, simple necessities,

and a Bible. The community wasn't sure what to make of this, and the preacher wasn't sure what to do next.

Marion and Dale knew. Marion Hale and Dale Lesher, lay members in the preacher's church, also befriended Ev. Exposure to Everett's daily suffering and encroaching peril was used by God's Spirit to nudge them toward involvement. Would they act decisively, or compromise?

They bought Everett new clothes and one Saturday took him to a school where Marion was employed. In the boys' locker room, Everett was taken to a shower stall, seated in a chair, and given his first head-to-foot bath in years. A scrub-brush was used because a washcloth with soap wasn't sufficient for 20 years of dirt. Can you imagine being filthy for so many years that you couldn't remember what it felt like to be clean? Dale, on his hands and knees, trimmed ten toenails. This was way beyond biblical foot-washing. The old garments were discarded, and Ev walked out of that building clean, in new clothes, and a step closer to a right mind. No one had thought of him at Christmas in twenty years. Now he received gifts of love and tasted Christian companionship. Authentic Christianity, anointed with beauty and grace, reached the "least of these my brothers and sisters" (Matthew 25:40, NLT).

> *Ev walked out of that building clean, in new clothes, and a step closer to a right mind.*

There remained the problem that Ev was essentially a homeless man in his own house. His frail health could not be expected to endure another winter without heat. Marion and Dale prayed for God's wisdom and provision and received an answer in the form of an idea. They moved into research mode, wrote letters, and made phone inquiries. *Eureka!* and *Praise the Lord!* Everett was due military veteran care of which he had no knowledge. Residence in a VA retirement home 50 miles away was secured, with Dale and Marion providing transportation. Ev resisted leaving his cave-like existence and his cats, but once in his new quarters, he never asked to return. Dale and Marion even cared for the cattle back home until they could be sold.

An amazing metamorphosis marked Ev's life over the following weeks. Without a wheelbarrow to push and with a little exercise therapy for his arthritis, Ev was again standing tall and straight. Bent over, he always seemed about four feet high. Now he stood face to face with others. The hermit discovered the pleasure of conversation, the value of friends, and the winsomeness of a smile and a wink. The nursing staff reported he had become the socialite of the resident home, making up for lonely, wasted years. The teacher's mind was coming back after having been misplaced for decades, and the VA chapel with hymns of faith became his eager delight.

> They entered into another's world with the love of Jesus, and it became a sacred adventure, a holy journey of pure pleasure.

Jesus had touched Everett and healed him, as surely as he restored people with disabilities to wholeness two thousand years ago. Dale and Marion were the hands, the feet, the body of Christ to walk into this man's experience with healing. They entered into another's world with the love of Jesus, and it became a sacred adventure, a holy journey of pure pleasure. The whole of Royal Center learned of Everett's transformation, and some believed in Jesus. God himself had come to town, and many responded to his love.

The apostle John tells of a group of Greeks who brought a request to Phillip. "Sir," they said, "we would like to see Jesus" (John 12:21, NIV). Royal Center saw Christ's love working through the hearts and hands of Marion and Dale.

Step one was exposure to and identity with ongoing suffering in their community. They quit pretending that if their own needs were met the world was at peace. No longer would Dale and Marion just mow their lawns, watch sports on television, and pretend that since they didn't see Everett's pain, it didn't exist. God doesn't require you to solve everyone's needs or fix everything that's broken. But are you willing to be Jesus' heart—to feel the affliction of someone, and as the Spirit leads, to be Jesus' healing hands?

The seventh promise could be stated: *With God's help, I promise to influence my neighbor and community world with the love of Jesus.* That world may be bigger than the one you thought you touched. Jesus' love through you to one person or family in your community may remain your secret act of kindness, or God may reveal it to the whole town and countryside, initiating a season of spiritual revival.

The world you touch may be even bigger than that— you may even touch Jesus. Our Lord taught, "I was hungry, and you fed me. . . . I was naked, and you gave me clothing" (Matthew 25:35–36). Bewildered, his friends couldn't remember such an occasion, and asked when they'd so served him. "When you did it to one of the least of these my brothers and sisters, you were doing it to me" (verse 40). Dale and Marion fed and clothed Everett and Jesus, too.

That's the wonder of touching the needy with love. You can fulfill both of the great commandments—a two-for-one bonus. When asked which was the most important commandment, Jesus answered, "Hear, O Israel, the Lord our God, the Lord is one. Love the Lord your God with all your heart and with all your soul and with all your mind and with all your strength. The second is this: Love your neighbor as yourself" (Mark 12:29–31). In loving their neighbor Everett, Dale and Marion also loved the Lord himself.

The Centurion's World

The church was committed to the 50-Day Spiritual Adventure, but before that event could begin, the pastor resigned and moved on to the Lord's new assignment for him. Denominational executives and retired clergy were found for Sunday preaching, but leadership for the Wednesday night church program fell to layperson Rudy Gehr. In this Lutheran church, Wednesdays during Lent were major events, with a full dinner for everyone and a Christ-honoring service. Rudy led the congregation through the 50-Day Spiritual Adventure, which included individual daily Bible study with journaling and spiritual disciplines called "Action Steps." Rudy would speak at the weekly preaching or teaching session.

As he prepared for the coming Wednesday's lesson, the thought came that he should disguise himself as a homeless person and enter the service late. The Adventure theme for the week was to practice welcoming others into the church as Christ would have received them. He would first monitor the reactions from the pews and then teach from the pulpit. The

Lord had much more dramatic plans for Rudy and the church.

Tuesday night before the Lenten service, Rudy received a phone call. "I'm a political refugee. My wife, children, and I are fleeing for our lives. A woman near the Canadian border said that if we made it to this town in the United States, I should call this phone number, and you would help us." This sounded more like a practical joke than political reality. It seemed preposterous that in civilized countries one should fear not for victory but for life itself. Being a Christian gentleman, and uncertain about the phone call, Rudy continued the conversation, asking pertinent questions.

The caller claimed he was the chief political officer of a foreign nation overseeing an embassy in Canada, and that he had courteously received opposition party members into the embassy. His government immediately recalled him, directed him to fly home, where the political realities were that he expected to be executed. "Will you help us?" was the plea.

> *His government immediately directed him to fly home, where he expected to be executed. "Will you help us?" was the plea.*

Should Rudy and the church reach out to this family, or should they shrug their shoulders and say, "This isn't our problem"?

What would Jesus do? Would he lift his hand to help an outsider, a foreigner, someone who spoke with inverted sentences and to our ears a strange accent? Would he snipe, "Why don't you go back where you came from?"

"When Jesus arrived in Capernaum, a Roman officer came and pleaded with him, 'Lord, my young servant lies in bed, paralyzed and racked with pain'" (Matthew 8:5–6).

This Roman officer held the rank of centurion. He didn't oversee the operations of the Roman embassy, but he may have been in charge of guarding it. Commanding one hundred occupying troops, he was a government employee sent in from Rome. Local sentiment, if followed, would have been against coming to this man's aid. The Jews of Palestine 2,000 years ago were as fervently nationalistic as they are in Israel today. This officer was not seen as just another outsider, but as the despised and hated enemy, the enforcer of Roman rule and revenue. Later, a centurion would be in charge of the crucifixion of our Lord. What would Jesus do this day? "Jesus said, 'I will come and heal him'" (verse 7).

If Jesus would help an officer of the oppressor, Rudy knew he could aid a refugee. Rudy and his wife welcomed this immigrant family into their home for the next several nights, even as the church welcomed them into their company. A man in the church with an empty house tied up in probate court offered it as home to the family for the next several months. The embassy family came eagerly to church and, having tasted the true love of Jesus, soon came to believe in him. After several months, employment was secured, and Rudy's refugee friends settled in, belonging to the church, the community, and to Jesus. What a great story!

On another front, the church I attend has taken up residence in a local community center, which serves a neighborhood where scores of languages are spoken. This neighborhood is more or less the Ellis

Island of Chicago's western suburbs. Together, the Outreach Community Center and Bridgeway Community Church serve those God has sent from every continent and many countries. Feeling sympathetic to newcomers' tensions and loneliness, problems, and often poverty, is a matter we all must continually work at. There are cultural barriers to be addressed, and in church there are issues about worship traditions that must be handled in humility. Every problem needs to be seen as an opportunity to be Christlike in love.

The Lord once explained, "I led them with cords of human kindness, with ties of love" (Hosea 11:4, NIV). Our acts of love, deeds of kindness, and exemplary Christian compassion are woven together into bridles and halters the Lord uses to lead others to himself. So I'm hoping you will resolve as a person of promise: *With God's help, I promise to influence the worlds of immigrants, refugees, and other new arrivals with the love of Jesus.*

The world you touch may be even bigger than that— you may even touch Jesus again. "I was a stranger and you invited me into your house" (Matthew 25:35). Rudy and the church housed refugees and Jesus, too. That's the wonder of touching newcomers in love.

The Suffering Church World

Two hundred ninety-two churches remain closed under Communist rule in Vietnam, according to the *Voice of the Martyrs* newsletter, with only eleven official churches still functioning. While that sounds like the death knell of the church, the brighter picture is that the "underground" church is growing daily. Christians with motorbikes ride up to twelve hours on muddy roads to lovingly share the Gospel with tribes that have never heard the name of Jesus.

They often travel at night to avoid run-ins with police.[1] It doesn't always work.

Vietnamese pastor Nguyen Lap Ma and his family have been under house arrest for fifteen years for refusing to give the Christian and Missionary Alliance Church at Can Tho to the Communists. Many other Vietnamese Christians are in prison for preaching the gospel illegally.

What would Jesus do for the persecuted church? What do the apostles say about caring for our suffering brothers and sisters? Are we allowed to cover our ears, squint our eyes, button our lips, and play "hear no evil, see no persecution, speak no sympathy"? The wider church is suffering in 38 nations under the most horrific persecution in history. Two million Christians have been killed in the 1990s in Sudan. Yet this pain and injustice is invisible to most until we follow it and make it our concern.

Do you know that vigilant and diligent care for the persecuted is a major biblical theme? Are you aware that much of the New Testament was written from prison cells, house arrest, or exile by heroes of persecution? The apostle Paul's survival while imprisoned was directly related to the care of Christians who determined to never forget him. There were times when that care grew thin, and Paul's endurance was at risk.

In his prison letter to the Philippian church, Paul speaks freely of how "his chains" turned to the benefit, instead of the hindrance, of the spread of the gospel (Philippians 1:12ff). His letter from prison to the Colossian believers commends the couriers, Tychicus and Onesimus, and extends greetings from fellow prisoner Aristarchus. He affirms the doctor, Luke, who tended his needs, and his companion

Mark. Paul's closing plea, eloquent in three words, was "Remember my chains" (Colossians 4:18, NIV). The bottom line is: "Remember those in prison as if you were their fellow prisoners, and those who are mistreated as if you were suffering" (Hebrews 13:3, NIV).

Chicago's Midway Airport is lacking all beauty and hospitable amenities. Its one redeeming quality is that ingress and egress are speedy—usually. My departure was delayed several hours in thirty-minute increments. The loudspeaker rasped, "The new departure time for flight 123 is 6:38

The only thing departing was my patient disposition and low blood pressure.

P.M.," then, "Flight 123 is now scheduled for a 7:08 P.M. departure." The only thing departing was my patient disposition and low blood pressure.

As I began to whine to God, "If I'm to speak for you tomorrow, you need to get me out of here now," his Spirit whispered, *Remember the persecuted who have been in prison for years. Pray for them.* I was simultaneously rebuked and redirected.

Midway, with its cement construction, narrow halls, cattle gates for people, and uniformed guards, could almost pass for a minimum-security prison—except that before the night was over, I would fly away. The Lord helped me transform gate B-7 from cell to chapel. The next two hours I prayed for children stolen from a Christian mother's breast in Sudan and sold into slavery. I prayed for imprisoned Cuban preachers and those they would speak to of Jesus' gospel. I prayed for converts in Pakistan and Saudi Arabia, for whom Christian baptism is not only a sign of new life but also a likely death warrant. My church small group leader is Nigerian, and I prayed through what I could remember of churches destroyed and Christians slaughtered in North Africa. I prayed for the World Evangelical Fellowship and Voice of the Martyrs, spokespeople for—and servants to—the persecuted church.

> *Since my Midway experience, I've encountered traffic jams, delayed meetings, and telephones "on hold." Each time I've prayed.*

Since my Midway experience, I've encountered traffic jams, delayed meetings, and telephones "on hold." Each time I've prayed for those not delayed but detained, not on hold but in the hold. When my doctor ran an hour late, I prayed for North Koreans, Christian or otherwise, who have nothing to eat. When frustrated getting everyone out the door for church, I prayed for Afghanistan Christians for whom there is no freedom of assembly.

Vietnamese pastor Nguyen Lap Ma and family have received 3,118 letters from Christians around the world.

> From the date the authorities allowed me to receive letters, after being forbidden for twelve years, I devour every letter we receive and meditate on the Scriptures shared in them. I then share these words of encouragement and the Scriptures . . . with my family. We are glad and encouraged in the spirit for the messages in them. I read them with prayers and tears, because I know our Father never will leave us nor forsake us. He has strengthened and helped us. So we keep hoping in Him and

fixing our eyes on Jesus, and following Him to endure the cross, scorning its shame to the point of death; when we are living, God uses us to comfort the other suffering Christians.[2]

Three thousand, one hundred eighteen Christians in the free world entered the sufferings of Pastor Nguyen Lap Ma and family and touched them with the love of Jesus. A family in Washington State held an open house in their home to collect Bibles, books, and blankets for Christians in Sudan. "This year for my twelfth birthday," writes Stephanie C. of Illinois, "instead of gifts, I asked my friends to bring donations for the children of Pakistan. It was a big success!"[3]

Resolve as a person of promise: *With God's help, I promise to influence the suffering world of persecuted brothers and sisters with the love of Jesus.* The world you touch may be even bigger than you think—you may even touch Jesus, who will be grateful because, "I was in prison and you visited me" (Matthew 25:36).

The World That Still Needs Jesus

Before Jesus went to the cross, he made a post-res-urrection appointment with his disciples. "After I have been raised from the dead, I will go ahead of you to *Galilee* and meet you there" (Matthew 26:32, italics added). Days later, on resurrection morning, an angel was sent to the empty tomb to meet and direct Mary Magdalene and another Mary. "Don't be afraid!" he said: "I know you are looking for Jesus who was crucified. He isn't here! He has been raised from the dead, just as he said would happen. Come, see where his body was lying. And now, go quickly and tell his disciples he has been raised from the dead, and he is going ahead of you to *Galilee*. You will see him there" (Matthew 28:5–7, italics added). This Galilean appointment appears significant in

Christ's agenda. As the two women hurried to find the disciples, they ran into the risen Lord himself. "Don't be afraid! Go tell my brothers to leave for *Galilee*, and they will see me there" (verse 10, italics added).

This Galilean meeting with the disciples was paramount to Jesus. Something momentous must have been planned for Galilee. What would it be?

"The eleven disciples left for Galilee, going to the mountain where Jesus had told them to go" (verse 16). Jesus made this appointment even before Calvary, and constantly reminded them to keep it. The tension mounted as they wondered what Jesus would do or say that was so important.

Jesus came and told his disciples,

> "I have been given complete authority in heaven and earth. Therefore, go and make disciples of all the nations, baptizing them in the name of the Father and the Son and the Holy Spirit. Teach these new disciples to obey all the commands I have given you. And be sure of this: I am with you always, even to the end of the age." (verses 18–20)

Instruction for reaching the world with the gospel was the one issue that occupied Jesus' attention. His Father loved the whole world, and so did he. And so should we, by resolving, *With God's help, I promise to influence the world of missions with the love of Jesus.*

Every book in the New Testament was written by a foreign missionary. Every letter in the New Testament was written to a convert of a foreign missionary, or a church planted by a missionary. Of the twelve apostles chosen by our Lord, all but one became a missionary. The one who didn't become a missionary became a traitor. The problems the early church wrestled with were largely questions of missionary procedure.

As you expand your vision beyond your fenced-in yard, your world will include your community, those God brings from other places, the persecuted church, and the world that still needs Jesus.

The other day I had breakfast with a man whose son is a missionary in Madras, India. He beamed with pride as he told of the wonders Christ is doing in that city. We must still be willing to bless our sons and daughters as they go to the farthest corner of the world. I'll respond this week to the fundraising letter of a friend who will be a short-term summer mission-

> *Every book in the New Testament was written by a foreign missionary. Every letter was written to a convert of a foreign missionary.*

ary in an African nation. She is the mother of two teens, and Dad will care for them, as Mom is obedient to the Galilean call. With transportation readily available, high school youth groups are regularly tasting distant mission service. Every teen I know who's visited a mission field has grown in his or her commitment to Christ. Three women in my town opened up a resale shop in a mall. All proceeds are dedicated to a mission program, and last year they supplied $80,000. The average western Christian only gives a penny a day to global missions. We can all do so much more if we believe in the Galilean priority.

Financial and prayer support for native home-grown missionaries is wise stewardship for most of us. K. P.

Yohannan oversees 10,000 Indian evangelists who preach in the villages. He would have us know:

> When Asians share Christ with other Asians in a culturally acceptable way, the results are startling. One of the native missionaries we support in northwest India, for example, now has evangelized sixty villages and established thirty churches in a difficult area of the Punjab. He has led hundreds to Christ. . . . He was living just like the people. He had only a one-room house made of dung and mud. . . . I discovered he spent two to three hours daily in prayer, reading and meditating on the Bible. This is what it takes to win Asia for Christ.[4]

Forty or fifty dollars will support such a missionary for a month.

In an age of satellites and CNN, of global e-mail and travel, are you expanding your world of Christian love and service? From neighbor to immigrant to suffering saint, from Nigeria to Indonesia to Sri Lanka, may we embrace Christ's Galilean vision: *With God's help, I promise to influence my world with the love of Christ.*

That's a promise worth keeping by a person of promise.

Love ever gives, forgives, outlives,
And ever stands with open hands,
And while it lives it gives,
For while it gives it lives,
And this is love's prerogative,
To give and give and give.
—*Author unknown*

"As I traveled, viewing the effects of pagan religions on India, I realized that the masses of India are starving because they are slaves to sin. The battle against hunger and poverty is really a spiritual battle, not a physical or social one as secularists would have us believe."

—*K. P. Yohannan*, Revolution in World Missions

Help me speak your fragrance wherever I go.
Flood my soul with your Spirit and life.
Penetrate and possess my whole being so utterly
   That my life may be only a radiance of yours.
Shine through me and be so in me that every soul I
   Come in contact with may feel your presence in
   My soul.
Let them look up,
And see no longer me,
   But only Jesus!
Amen
—*Mother Teresa of Calcutta*

CHAPTER 8

Reaching the Goal

*With God's help, I promise to live one day at a time
through the power of the risen Christ.*

Thump, thump, thump. It was the unmistakable reso-
nance of a basketball on a cement driveway. The
bounce of the ball was a frequent happy sound
when my son lived at home. When Larry and his
friends made the thump sounds, we also heard
laughter, the scuffle of shoes, and "Foul! You can't
hit me like that." Without painted lines, obvious
boundaries, and referees, driveway basketball was as
much a battle of wits and negotiation as athletic
prowess. But for the past three years, Larry had lived
200 miles away on a college campus. To the neighbor's joy and my melancholy, the backyard thump
had been silenced.

There it was again—*thump, thump, thump*—but with no
yelling or clang of the rim. Curiosity being one of
my better qualities, I could not ignore this. Spying
through the kitchen window, I gazed upon the most
beautiful sight—my granddaughter, Gini, had rescued
the basketball from garage oblivion and was practicing dribbling. The sport survived, the baton had
been passed—"Long live driveway basketball!"—to
the hands of a six-year-old girl.

She obviously needed coaching, and what's a grand-pa for, if not coaching? Grandpas don't yell, spank, or scold—they listen, praise, and coach. I'd coached her on how to take a snow sled and, with a running start, flop on it for a great downhill winter ride. Now here was an opportunity for summer bonding and coaching.

"Gini, show me how you make a basket."

"I can't—it's too high," she wistfully answered, looking toward the day when she would be taller and stronger.

Here's my opportunity to be a hero, I thought. *She can't make a basket because she never had a coach.* Since she was only six, this would require a two-handed push shot. I demonstrated my inglorious form, and after no more than six or eight shots, one clattered through the rim. I handed her the ball, which she gallantly threw at least two and a half feet straight up. After the tears (from the ball rattling her chin after bounding off her head) stopped, I gave her the ball again. Being an astute Lupton grandchild, she didn't repeat the same mistake. This time, the ball went straight forward, never reaching head height elevation, and fell harmlessly half a body length away from her.

A lesser coach would have packed it in about then. But Grandpa hadn't run out of ideas. "Take the ball in both hands and hold it between your legs. Then sweep it up, underhand style." Again I demonstrated, and about the time she was ready to run off with another game, a shot swished through the goal. "Now it's your turn, Gini." This was by far her most powerful attempt. The ball flew over her head back-wards, landing in the neighbor's petunias on the other side of the fence.

Fearing she would hate basketball forever, I did the only decent thing a grandpa could do. I hoisted her to my shoulders, and from there she finally had the joy of putting the ball through the hoop. Twice was enough for my back. "One more, pleeeease," she begged. I'd become a victim of my own success—she wanted to live on my shoulders and shoot baskets. I tried to reason the benefits of coloring books and paper dolls, but these wouldn't do. She was hooked on hoops. So I found one more grandpa trick. With a ladder and a couple of wrenches I shimmied the backboard and rim down the post to about six feet high. Ten minutes later the backyard was filled with the screeches of a dozen neighborhood children shooting hoops and whooping it up. Third and fourth graders were ecstatic at being "like Mike" and playing above the rim.

> *Fearing she would hate basketball forever, I did the only decent thing a grandpa could do. I hoisted her to my shoulders.*

Up till now, in this book, we've been digging the hole, placing the post, pouring the concrete, and hanging the backboard. We've established the goal. The "nothing but net" goal is Christian authenticity rather than perfection. Living less imperfectly is the long-range, three-point goal we're hoping for.

One or two readers are thinking this is lay-up easy: *I can keep these promises for the rest of my life without enough effort to wind me.* Water-skiing, mothering, and playing the flute also look easy to the uninitiated.

Others are thinking, *I've got the family and friends promises down pat, but the church and showing God's love promises will take all the effort I can muster. It's a big mountain, but like the little engine in the children's story, "I think I can, I think I can."*

More than a few are protesting, *The goal's too high. I feel like your granddaughter—try as I do, I'm always three feet short of the target. You'll either have to put me on your shoulders or lower the goal.*

While I have no intention of lowering God's standard, I do have good news for you. There is more good news in Christ's gospel than most of us ever discern.

News Bulletin #1

Good News Bulletin #1 reads, "Being in the game counts." The moment Gini pulled the orange ball from the hidden garage treasures and began to dribble, she was more in the basketball process than someone with Laker season tickets who doesn't touch a ball.

Anyone who has moved from spectator critic to Christian participant has reason to stand tall. Chicago's newspapers employ many of the best writers in the business. The automotive writers report the shortcomings of any and every vehicle. The arts reviewers demoralize musicians with caustic commentary. The sports writers revel in criticizing flawed athletic performances. What most critics don't do is build cars, act in plays, or score touchdowns.

Christianity has enough critics and spectators. By claiming the seven promises as your own, you've come out of the stands and onto the stage or the playing field.

The Scripture words that describe the Christian life are words of process rather than end result: *walk*,

*run, seek, follow, grow, wrestle, pray, confess, beware, contin-
ue, wait, read, fight, endure, watch.* These words introduce instruction for the trip, not the destination.
Grow in grace, walk in the Spirit, and *wait on the Lord* are
process words for life's journey.

"Allison receives a ribbon for faithful attendance.
Cindy receives the 'ready to help' certificate.
Zachary wins the award for the boy with the most
energy." I was guest speaker for a church youth club
award night and observer of a church with wisdom.
Any child committed to the process heard his or her
name called, marched proudly to the front, and
received recognition with applause. Leadership
might have saved time and expense by awarding tro-
phies to the three highest
achievers in the church club
program. But they chose to
love and affirm 100 percent of
the clubbers. Any youngster
involved in the club program
was honored. No child, however, received an award for
reading about the club, or
being a friend of a clubber, or
thinking about joining, or
dropping out.

> *In making the seven
> promises, you've
> entered the process
> of becoming the man
> or woman God
> wants you to be.*

In making the seven promises, you've entered the
process of becoming the man or woman God wants
you to be. You've come face-to-face with values and
responsibilities and commitments. You've chosen to
be included in God's program. And God affirms all
in the process toward maturity and Christian
authenticity.

Fred Hartley remembers, "When I was in high
school, I met Jesus. One night, alone in my own
room, I got down on my knees and prayed a very

simple prayer. I said: 'Jesus, I believe that when you died on the cross, you died for my sins. And I believe that you also rose from the dead and that you are alive right now. I open my heart and ask you to come in and make me a new person. Thank you, Jesus!'"

Fred continues,

> Today I am convinced that Christianity without commitment is a sure loser. The greatest decision one will ever make is: What should I do with Jesus? I have come to the conclusion there are only two options: reject him completely, or follow him 100 percent. Christianity is either worth everything, or it isn't worth a gum wrapper![1]

Because it's worth everything, you've decided to make some promises, to strive for authenticity, to get in the process, to become genuine gold rather than fool's gold. Christ honors those in the process of growth and maturity.

Instead of compromising, you've entered the process resolving, *With God's help, I promise to live one day at a time through the power of the risen Christ.*

News Bulletin #2

Good News Bulletin #2 announces, "All Christ's biddings include his enablings." I asked Gini to shoot the basket, but she didn't have the strength. So I held her on my shoulders to make it possible for her to put the ball through the hoop. If you wonder whether you can reach Christ's goal and keep the seven promises, the answer is that whatever Jesus expects of you he enables you to do. That's why each promise has the preface "With God's help."

Jesus went to the synagogue, where he noticed a

man with a deformed hand. After a minor skirmish with the Pharisee critics who were to real religion what sports critics are to basketball players, Jesus said to the man, "Stretch out your hand." So he stretched it out (Matthew 12:13, NIV). Jesus never asked anyone to do anything without adding his strength.

"Come forth," Jesus said to Lazarus, "and he that was dead came forth" (John 11:43–44, KJV). Lazarus, who'd died several days earlier, had no power in himself to walk out of the tomb. But Jesus' biddings include his enablings.

Jesus and the disciples were in a boat on the Sea of Galilee when an unusually fierce and frightening storm rose up. Jesus "rebuked the wind, and said to the sea, 'Peace, be still.' And the wind ceased, and there was a great calm" (Mark 4:39, KJV). Can the wind cease in mid-blow? Can the waves flatten out in a moment? They can if Jesus so instructs them, because all his biddings include his enablings.

> *If Freddie Fritz says, "Come," you'd better have a lifejacket on. But when Jesus bids, "Come," you will be able to accomplish his calling.*

To a man with a 38-year-long crippling handicap, Jesus said, "'Get up! Pick up your mat and walk.' At once the man was cured; he picked up his mat and walked" (John 5:8, NIV). From that I conclude that when Christ's word for me is to make family relationships a priority or address a hidden prejudice, his bidding includes his enabling.

The disciples saw Jesus walking on the water but, having never witnessed such a sight, weren't sure if it was really

149

Jesus or a ghost. Peter spoke up, "Lord, if it's you, tell me to come to you on the water."

Jesus answered with the monosyllabic direction, "Come."

"Then Peter got down out of the boat, walked on the water and came toward Jesus" (Matthew 14:28-29, NIV). If Freddie Fritz says "Come," you'd better have a lifejacket on, because you won't walk on water. But when Jesus bids, "Come," "teach," "love," or "go," rest assured in your heart that you will be able to accomplish his calling, because all Christ's biddings come packaged with his enablings.

"I pray that you will begin to understand the incredible greatness of his power for us who believe him. This is the same mighty power that raised Christ from the dead" (Ephesians 1:19-20). The power of the Resurrection is the power that enables any Christian to walk away from slavish bondage to a signature sin (Romans 6:7). "I can't" doesn't hold water. Christ's resurrection power makes "I can't" an empty protest.

I bought a Walkman-style radio/cassette player with the package clearly labeled, *Batteries not included*. I have the special gift of overlooking the obvious, so I inserted a cassette and pushed the command button, *Play*. Nothing happened, nothing moved, nothing sang. Any command Christ gives to you through his Word, the counsel of a friend or book, or by his Spirit, comes with batteries included. All his biddings include his enablings.

So, depending on his enabling, repeat the final promise with me: *With God's help, I promise to live one day at a time through the power of the risen Christ.*

Good News Bulletin #3

Good News Bulletin #3 is "Each day is a new game."
I didn't want Gini to shoot baskets in the driveway
for the rest of her life. I just wanted her to shoot
baskets that day. You don't have to think about
keeping these seven promises for the rest of your
life. An authentic person of promise gives attention
to just one day—this day.

I wonder if I'll ever hear an athlete boast, "Today's
game doesn't matter. I'm looking forward to the
game next month." They never say that. No matter
how strong their own team, or how weak the oppo-
nent, every coach and con-
testant strictly maintains,
"When next week comes,
we'll face its challenges. The
only thing that matters today
is today's game." The writer
of the Jim Carrey movie *Liar,
Liar* instinctively knew better
than to have the young son
wish that his dad would stop
telling lies forever. The story
was limited to a wish for just
one day without a lie.

> *"When next week
> comes, we'll face its
> challenges. The only
> thing that matters
> today is today's
> game."*

"I fulfill my vows day by day" was David's approach
to success before God and in his kingly duties
(Psalm 61:8). The seven promises of this book have
transformed churches, families, relationships, neighborhoods, and personal character and spirituality.
The transformation hasn't been once and for all, but
one day at a time. Like the recovering alcoholic at
an AA meeting, success is measured by how we live
today. After months of victory, we may rejoice, "I've
been sober for five months and nine days." Success,
however, isn't measured in five-month increments
but by fulfilling vows day by day.

Even Jesus, who clearly knew his purpose in coming to earth, went in prayer to his Father in heaven for instructions one day at a time. Would you be surprised to learn that there are over 2,500 mentions of "day" and "daily" in the Bible? Living for God a day at a time is a major biblical theme.

"Give us this day our daily bread," Jesus taught his disciples to pray (Matthew 6:11, KJV). As a youngster, that part of the Lord's Prayer annoyed me. I understood that bread could mean wheat bread or rice bread or even meat and potatoes. I even knew bread could mean clothing and shelter. The prayer is for basic needs and the minimum daily need is something healthy to eat. The part that annoyed me was the "daily" word. Why couldn't I pray for a month or a year at a time? Yet "daily" has always been part of God's plan. During the wilderness journey following the exodus from Egypt, God supplied Israel with manna to eat on a daily basis. I must trust Christ to supply all of my needs one day at a time.

"Each day he carries us in his arms" (Psalm 68:19). Christ's biddings are his enablings, *on a daily basis*. This is God's grace—he daily provides, enables, guides, and strengthens. "As thy days, so shall thy strength be" (Deuteronomy 33:25, KJV).

We must daily appropriate this grace. The psalmist said, "I cry unto thee daily" (Psalm 86:3, KJV). The Christians at Berea "searched the Scriptures daily" (Acts 17:11, KJV). Jesus taught his followers to take up one's "cross daily and follow me" (Luke 9:23, KJV). Daily habits for the person of promise include prayer, Bible study, and submission of the will to the Lord.

Will you agree that all the objections and excuses against living the seven promises have been addressed and satisfied in Jesus? He wants you to step into the game—or process—of being a person of promise. Whatever he wants for you, he enables. This day is the only day that requires your focus.

News Bulletin #4

But what if, in spite of Christ's resurrection power, I mess up? What if, like Gini, I shoot for the goal and come up short? What if I get discouraged with myself and feel like walking away?

Good News Bulletin #4 is "Mercy means a restart." If you failed at a hundred diets, you can start again tomorrow. If you struck out ten times in a row, the next time at bat can be a home run. Many business successes follow repeated failures. Never say quit, especially in being an authentic Christian. Quitting is the ultimate compromise.

> *Illinois legislators may not be aware of it, but the clean plate rule comes right out of Scripture. It's God's rule for starting a new day.*

I felt sorry for the owner, letting my son in at half price. A few six-year-old boys like Larry could eat Grandma's Buffet out of business. Larry took an adult-size plate and filled it high and wide with every kind of morsel a lad enjoys. Neither of our children were picky eaters, a quality learned early from Mom's good cooking. Her farm-acquired "eat it or go hungry" attitude to what she served from the kitchen may have contributed in some small measure to Larry's sensible approach to food.

As Larry balanced and carried his troughlike plate to our table, men and women gawked, chuckled, and commented, "Whatcha gonna do with all that food,

little guy? Your eyes are bigger than your belly."
Twenty minutes later, Larry arrogantly strutted past
these naysayers with his empty plate. Refill time was
when the real fun began.

The buffet bar's attendant nearly broke my son's
heart as he took the empty plate out of his hands.
"You can't bring that plate back to the bar, Sonny,"
he sternly ordered. Larry knew his rights, so he
stood up to him.

"This is an all-you-can-eat restaurant. My dad said I
could have seconds," he whimpered.

The attendant softened, "Sure you can, young man.
But the State has a law that you can't bring a dirty
plate back to the buffet line. Germs might spread.
The rule is that I give you a clean plate each time
you want more food. Here's your new plate. Enjoy!"
(They always command, "Enjoy!")

Illinois legislators may not be aware of it, but the
clean plate rule comes right out of Scripture. It's
God's rule for starting a new day. "Great is his faithfulness; his mercies begin afresh each day" (Lamen-
tations 3:23). Mercies are for the mess-ups, the sins
and failures of life. Mercy means it's always too early
to be discouraged or quit.

At the end of the day, it's a good habit to thank God
for all the ways he ministered to you or through
you, for all his power in helping you be a person of
promise. And the sins and disappointments, the
"shouldas and couldas" of the day, you admit or
confess to God (1 John 1:8–10).

But my memory is selectively poor, and I forget to
confess all the ways in which I've been less than
Jesus wanted of me that day. I rejoice in this—the

next morning his mercies are as fresh as his grace.
Yesterday's misses and messes aren't allowed at
today's table. Daily grace starts me off with fresh
power. Daily mercy hands me a clean plate.

Here is the approach to being an authentic person
of promise: Get in the game, believe in Christ's
enabling power, and live one day at a time. You'll
soon be so excited about life that you'll never want
to put the ball down. Like a granddaughter squeez-
ing the moments of twilight, you'll be calling out,
"One more shot, pleeease." And the Lord's smiling
answer will be, "Tomorrow's another day."

*With God's help, I promise to live one day at a time through
the power of the risen Christ.*

That's a promise worth keeping by people of
promise.

"The sanctification of the daily life means sanctification of the whole life."
—*Anonymous*

I heard a voice at evening softly say,
    "Bear not thy yesterday into tomorrow;
Nor load this week with last week's load of sorrow.
    Lift all thy burdens as they come, nor try
To weight the present with the by and by.
    One step, and then another, take thy way—
        Live by the day."
—*Julia Harris May*

"Tomorrow is God's secret—but today is yours to live."
—*Anonymous*

"Live What I Believe"
by Deborah Anders Koenigsberg, 1998

I believe in you.
I believe that you gave me life.
I believe that you've shown me, in your Word, how
  to live.
Help me, Jesus, to live what I believe.

Lord, help me to walk with you.
Just as you keep your promises, help me keep mine.
Help me to share the good news of your love and
  salvation.
Help me to give what I can't keep for myself alone.
Help me to see, with your eyes, the needs of all
  people.
Help me to love as you love, with a heart that is
  pure.

I believe in you.
I believe that you gave me life.
I believe that you've shown me, in your Word, how
  to live.
Help me, Jesus, to live what I believe.

Chapter 1: The Ultimate Knowledge
1. Richard Wurmbrand, *In God's Underground*, Living Sacrifice Book Company, Bartlesville, Okla., 1993, page 231.
2. Ibid., page 232.

Chapter 2: Authenticity Through Imprinting
1. Robert Horwich, *The ICF Bugle*, Baraboo, Wis., Vol. 12, Number 4, 1986.
2. Howard Hendricks, *Seven Promises of a Promise Keeper*, Focus on the Family Publications, Colorado Springs, Colo., 1994, page 53.
3. Patrick F. McManus, *A Fine and Pleasant Misery*, Owl Books, New York, 1978, pages 46–47.
4. *Eerdman's Handbook to Christianity in America*, Eerdmans Publishing, Grand Rapids, Mich., 1983, page 28.

Chapter 3: Signature List
1. John Henry Jowlett, *My Daily Meditation*, Grosset & Dunlap, New York, 1914, page 177.
2. Donald Grey Barnhouse, *God's Grace*, Eerdmans Publishing, Grand Rapids, Mich., 1982, page 71.

Chapter 4: The Family Story
1. Delores Curran, *Traits of a Healthy Family*, Ballantine Books, New York, 1987, page 227.
2. Ibid., page 242. (Not a direct quote.)

Chapter 6: Something In My Eye
1. James Stalker, *The Ethics of Jesus*, Hoddert & Stroughton, London, 1909, pages 289–290.
2. Mike Imrem, *Daily Herald*, Chicago, Tuesday, March 17, 1998, Section 2, page 1.
3. Ron Sider, *Genuine Christianity*, Zondervan Publishing House, Grand Rapids, Mich., 1996, page 75.
4. Ibid., page 102.
5. John M. Perkins, *Restoring At-Risk Communities*, Baker Book House, Grand Rapids, Mich., 1995, page 116.

Chapter 7: To The Worlds With Love
1. *Voices of the Martyrs*, Bartlesville, Okla., 1997 Special Issue, page 13.
2. Ibid., page 14.
3. *Voices of the Martyrs*, April 1998, page 13.
4. K.P. Yohannan, *Revolution in World Missions*, Creation House, Atlamonte Springs, Fla., 1992, pages 182–183.

Chapter 8: Reaching the Goal
1. Fred Hartley, *100%*, Fleming H. Revell Company, Old Tappan, N.J., 1983, page 13.

 **Dan Lupton** is a proven pastor, excellent preacher and motivational speaker, and committed Christian leader with strong intents to win souls to Christ and strengthen the church. From pastoring youth in Michigan to serving as a missionary and church planter in Utah to ministering over the radio waves in Indiana and serving as director of the Greater Chicago Sunday School Association in Illinois, this author has been involved with God's people in North America!

Currently, as Conference Ministries Director and speaker for Mainstay Church Resources, Dan oversees the setting up of conferences and serves as a seminar presenter for pastors across the continent who want to boost spiritual growth in their congregations. He also ministers to the church at large though Lupton Church Consulting and Bibles Direct.

Dan and his wife, Nancy, have been married for more than 30 years. They live in the town of Wheaton, Illinois, and enjoy reading, gardening, antiquing, and most of all spending time with their son, Larry, daughter, Amy, son-in-law, Tom, and grandchildren, Gini and Zachary.

Don't Miss Out on This Great Companion!

While *People of Promise* stands on its own, it's meant to be paired with a daily journal that helps you live what you believe for 50 days—just long enough to build healthy spiritual habits that last a lifetime!

Packed with Scripture explorations, life-application questions, and innovative action steps that will help you enjoy implementing five life-changing spiritual disciplines, the *Promises Worth Keeping: Resolving to Live What We Say We Believe* Adult Journal is part of the "PK" 50-Day Spiritual Adventure.

Get this exciting resource and resolve to take 15 minutes a day to develop your spiritual life. You'll find that a promise worth keeping!

Specs: 80 page saddle stitch—ISBN 1-57849-104-5, $6.99

To order, call Mainstay Church Resources at 1-800-224-2735 or contact your local Christian bookstore.

If you've enjoyed this book, you'll want to read:

I Like Church, But . . .
by Dan Lupton
Introduction by David R. Mains

If you dream about being part of a church that reaches its potential, you can do something to make that happen! Dan Lupton's other popular book, *I Like Church, But . . . ,* is filled with motivational illustrations and practical helps for becoming a part of the church you've always longed for.

Available in book or audio guidebook format, the eight chapters of *I Like Church, But . . .* will lead you to look more deeply at your attitudes and actions toward your church and help you focus on Christ and his goals for his church. "Make It Happen" action steps for individuals, families, and entire congregations are also included to help you strengthen your church in the eyes of Christ, his body of believers, and the world.

Specs: 198-page mass market—ISBN 1-56043-183-0, $5.99; approx. 120-minute audio guidebook—ISBN 1-57849-005-7, $11.99

To order, call Mainstay Church Resources at 1-800-224-2735 or contact your local Christian bookstore.